Illustrated History of the Third Reich

Illustrated History of the Third Reich

Alex Hook

Published by TAJ Books 2004

27, Ferndown Gardens,
Cobham,
Surrey,
UK,
KT11 2BH

All notations of errors or omissions (author inquiries, permissions) concerning the content of this book should be addressed to TAJ Books 27, Ferndown Gardens, Cobham, Surrey, UK, KT11 2BH, info@tajbooks.com.

ISBN 1-84406-030-6

Printed in China.
1 2 3 4 5 08 07 06 05 04

Contents

INTRODUCTION

The sudden end of World War I came as a shock to the German people—not only had they unexpectedly lost the war itself, but the national economy was in turmoil and the political situation was dire. In October 1918 soldiers and sailors had mutinied in their home barracks, and workers had formed militant union councils. Within two weeks there was revolution and a republic was declared. This caused the abdication of the Kaiser, which marked the end of the Hohenzollern dynasty. In its wake came a military dictatorship led by Erich Ludendorff and Paul von Hindenburg. On November 11, an armistice was declared and World War I came to an abrupt end.

On January 18, 1919, the Paris Peace Conference began, and the allies were in no mood to let the Germans off lightly. The price exacted for Germany going to war was not only financial, but geographical. This was partly in recompense for the massive loses suffered, but was also an attempt to stabilise the area to foster a long-lasting peace in Europe. The result of the reparations imposed was that the German economy collapsed—inflation spread like wild-fire, and those who had their life savings held in bank accounts lost everything.

A new German National Assembly was elected on January 19, 1919, but because Berlin was suffering from riots and other violent disorders, they met for the first time in Weimar. This new government was in fact a coalition of the three main parties—the SPD, DDP, and Centre under the chancellorship of Philipp Scheidemann. Shortly after this the National Assembly elected Friedrich Ebert (SPD) to be the first President of the Republic.

The Unknown Warrior's coffin resting in Westminster Abbey, in London, November 9, 1920. The carnage of World War I left most Europeans prepared to do anything to stop another war.

While the allies argued to and fro over the terms of the peace settlement, Germany's mainstream politics were in a state of disarray. Having been ruled by the Kaiser and his dynasty for many generations, the new political parties were still very immature, and the Socialists suffered from factional power plays which threatened their very survival. Chief amongst the radical elements were the Spartacists, who were for outright communism and supported Lenin and the Bolsheviks—they wanted a full radical revolution, and brought about a series of major public disorders in an attempt to bring down the government of the elected President, Friedrich Ebert. Midway between the radicals and the middle of the road socialists were the Independent Socialists who operated by organising all manner of demonstrations, strikes, and putsches, and were not at all interested in maintaining the status quo.

As a result of these threats to the government, Ebert was forced to turn to the army for direct support, which he achieved by reaching agreement with General Wilhelm Groener. To back this up, Ebert then got one of his Socialist colleagues, Gustav Noske, to create a paramilitary unit called the Free Corps (*Freikorps*).

This force was supported by the army, and provided the much needed muscle that was desperately needed to suppress the violence that the radicals were using on the streets throughout Germany.

The Spartacists tried to move on the government by taking Berlin, but the Free Corps went into action and secured many of the key strategic positions before eventually defeating them. The two main Spartacist leaders were captured and executed, and German politics settled down once again.

While the establishment of a new government may have given the German people some comfort, the allies were still working out the level of reparations they were going to impose. In April 1919, a figure of £5.4 billion was proposed—this was a staggering sum for the time. There was still much resentment amongst the German military, and when they realised that they were going to have to hand over their navy to the allies, they scuttled their entire fleet at Scapa Flow in June 1919, days before the Versailles Treaty was signed.

One of the biggest obstacles the treaty had to overcome in finding a permanent solution to the troubles in the region was that Germany and

M. Clemenceau, the French Prime Minister, leaving the Chateau at Versailles after the Peace Treaty had been signed, January 1, 1919.

Armistice Day outside Buckingham Palace: a vast crowd cheers the royal family on the balcony.

for it to work.

When it came on June 28, 1919, the Versailles Treaty was a devastating blow to Germany—it had to hand over large amounts of territory to its neighbours. Poland took the Polish Corridor and Silesia, France got the Alsace-Lorraine region, and other areas were given to Belgium and Denmark. Something else that sowed the seeds of bitter resentment in many people was that Germany was not allowed to unite with Austria. In order to reduce

Above: A happy crowd in Paris wave the Stars and Stripes and the French flag.
Below: The victorious Allies on the steps of Marshal Foch's special train in the forest of Compiègne where the Armistice was signed.

France were not only situated next to each other, they had a history of fighting each other stretching back into the mists of time. The most prosperous area in the Franco-German borders lay along the route of the River Rhine—this was not only significant for trade, but also for strategic purposes. The river itself is so large that it has been a natural defence line for thousands of years. For an army to cross it without using bridges would be a major task, and so the French were keen to see the Rhineland become a natural buffer to German aggression. France also had designs on Germany's steel and coal industries in the area which had a far greater output than her own. It was proposed that an independent state was created to achieve this, and as with any territorial dispute, there were native inhabitants both for and against the idea. When it came to the crunch, however, even with the French offering a 'no reparations' settlement, the separatists were too few in number

the possibility of Germany becoming a military threat in the future, its army was also limited to a maximum of 100,000 men.

When France was given the Alsace-Lorraine region, it got Germany's Saar valley—the French coal mining industry had been all but completely destroyed during the war, and so they were given the Saar valley (which was a premier coal mining area) in recompense. Although they didn't manage to get an independent state created, the French did get the concession that the Rhineland would be occupied by Allied troops for fifteen years—after which it would become a demilitarised zone. They also managed to get the Americans and British to make a guarantee that they would come to her aid should Germany try to invade France again.

After 47 years under German rule the French cavalry are joyously greeted in Strasbourg.

A searchlight belonging to the French army of occupation on the Rhine opposite St. Goar.

Although it seemed that a settlement had been reached that would create sufficient stability for a long-lasting European peace, the power-brokers overlooked a vital factor—that the German people as a whole believed that they hadn't lost the war in the true military sense, but that instead they'd been betrayed by the politicians. Had Germany been occupied by invading troops, the people may have felt differently, but for the vast majority the end of the war came as a remote, anticlimactic event. It is not clear just how this feeling could have been overcome at the time, but in ignoring it, the politicians allowed a wound to fester, something that would return to haunt the world within twenty years.

On top of the geographical losses, Germany also had to make reparations payments of £1 billion, and was made less significant on the world political

The Allies discuss the Armistice in October 1918: the swingeing terms would lead to great discontent in postwar Germany.

Crowds cheer British cavalry as they enter Spa on November 28, 1919.

stage by being barred from the League of Nations. There were many reasons why the reparations favoured France so heavily—having had their population decimated by the enormous human cost of the series of wars led by Napoleon, they could ill afford to fight another with Germany. On top of this, World War I killed off a large proportion of the males of fighting age, as well as significant numbers of civilians. Where once the two nations were of similar sizes, France now only had two thirds of Germany's population, which, to make matters worse was increasing at a dramatic rate. This meant that in the post-war era, the French had fallen a long way behind their aggressive neighbour in the power stakes, both militarily and economically.

While the French were doing their best to get the most out of the peace settlement, the Americans and British were concerned that France may end up too powerful, which would have been just as bad for stability as if Germany retained power. What was need was a balance, but this was not proving easy to establish.

As an immediate challenge to the power of the peace treaty, on September 12, 1919, a small Italian military force seized the town of Fiume—what is now the city of Rijeka on the Dalmatian coast. This small expeditionary force was led by a maverick who acted

The German fleet was scuttled at Scapa Flow on June 21, 1919 (this is the Hindenburg*). This would mean that the Nazis would have to start building a navy from scratch.*

without authority. After ruling the town through martial law for a year, he was forced out when he became too much of an embarrassment to the Italian government. While this episode is almost insignificant when viewed at the global level, it did highlight the inadequacies of the existing regulatory system.

As a forerunner to the creation of the United Nations, the League of Nations was intended to engender world peace, however, in many ways it was little more than a political road-show. The first full meeting took place in January 1920, but every nation that belonged to it had the power of veto, and some of the biggest players, including America, refused to join. Consequently, any pacts made under its auspices were barely worth the paper they were written on. This left France in a tricky position—although there was a League of Nations guarantee of her safety, the French pushed for the Treaty of Versailles to include a clause to provide military backing should Germany threaten her borders again. While this may have seemed to settle France's security concerns, the American Congress couldn't agree on the terms of the treaty, and failed to sign up to it, leaving the matter unresolved.

Although the peace settlement had made the Rhineland a demilitarised zone, in April 1920 the German government sent troops in to the area to quell rioting—this infuriated the French, who then invaded the Ruhr themselves. A month later they withdrew under pressure from the Americans and British.

The final level of financial reparations still hadn't been set, and once the League of Nations got involved, they argued back and forth for more than a year. On April 25, 1920, a figure of £4.5 billion was proposed—this was lower than had been suggested a year earlier, and so was rejected. In June the figure was raised to £12.5 billion—this amount was totally impractical, and after another six months of argument it was lowered to £10 billion, but this still failed to be accepted. The German delegation dug their heels in to try and get the figure lowered considerably, and in March 1921 in desperation at the way things were going, British, French and Belgian troops invaded the Ruhr to force Germany to toe the line.

With the presence of an allied military force in the Rhineland, the German delegation was more amenable, and the sum for reparations was finally agreed by all concerned at £6.6 billion—to be paid in instalments until 1984. To make sure that the agreement was taken seriously, allied troops stayed in place until the end of September. To the common people, however, this occupation created a huge amount of resentment, and while the world players were virtually playing chess with the map of Europe, a then unheard of Adolf Hitler joined a small political party in Munich called the German Workers Party—this was later to become the National Socialist German Workers Party, or Nazi Party.

Hitler and the Growth of the Nazi Party

Just how Adolf Hitler became to be so influential in German politics needs some explanation; he was born on April 20, 1889—a sickly baby, he was doted on by his over-protective mother. His father, however, was an abusive tyrant, who made his childhood and teenage years very difficult. His stubborn will earned him many beatings from his father—this left him with a sense of repressed anger, something that in his adult years easily spilled over into dramatic rages.

In the early years of schooling, Hitler was a good pupil, but as things became more difficult at home, he turned into a lazy, disinterested student. The only person who could hold his attention was his history teacher, Dr. Leopold Poetsch, who was a fervent Pan-German nationalist. The Pan-Germans believed in the superiority of the Aryan race, and that the strength of the German culture came from a strong, healthy, rustic lineage. They also believed that the Jews were an inferior race, as were many of the other Eastern European peoples, such as the Slavs. Dr. Poetsch's beliefs had a huge influence on Hitler, and later these ideas became a main component in his political campaigns.

Hitler's laziness at school meant that he had a complete lack of qualifications when he left—he had ambitions of becoming an artist, but when he applied to the various arts academies in Vienna, he was told that he wasn't good enough and that he wasn't qualified. When his mother died in 1907, Hitler was grief stricken, and inconsolable. The combination of this loss with his repressed anger meant that he was now a very bitter young man. When he read that the Jews were scheming to

Hitler and Goebbels are greeted off an aircraft in the 1930s.

Hitler at a memorial to the fallen in Hiltpoltstein, northern Bavaria.

destroy German culture and to achieve world domination, he believed every word. He further read that they were in league with the Catholics, Freemasons, and Jehovah's Witnesses, which riled him. He began talking of these matters with his friends, and such was the mass appeal of the message, he soon found himself at the centre of an admiring throng. He lapped up the attention, and started searching out more racist material to bolster his standing in this new social circle.

In 1914 Hitler was arrested for failing to register for military duty, but on medical screening was found to be too weak to bear arms, and so escaped service. His attitude seems to have changed after the Austrian Archduke Francis Ferdinand was assassinated, however, since he suddenly volunteered for military duty. In August he joined the 16th Bavarian Reserve Infantry Regiment, and saw his first action two months later, 5 miles east of Ypres. Shortly after this he was made a messenger to his unit's headquarters, but this didn't stop him being awarded the Iron Cross 2nd Class within a month.

The next couple of years were not particularly spectacular for Hitler; in 1915 he was made up to Lance Corporal, and in October 1916 he received a leg wound at the Somme, after which he spent two months in a military hospital near Berlin. He was wounded again in 1917, although it was only minor. When he returned to service, he saw action at Picardy, the Ypres Salient and at the infamous Passchendaele.

As the war drew to a close, he was awarded the Iron Cross 1st Class for his service as messenger a since 1914. Not long after this, his life was spared by a British soldier who couldn't bring himself to shoot a wounded man—this event was later seen by Hitler as a divine intervention that showed he was indeed fated to lead the world. A further incident that shaped his view of warfare—and ultimately worked in favour of the allies during World War II, was that in October 1918, Hitler was gassed and temporarily blinded. This effected him both physically and emotionally—years later when he came to power he refused to allow gas to be

Hitler toured the country extensively in the 1920s and 1930s, usually in a Mercedes.

used by his armed forces. This meant that for moral reasons the allies couldn't use chemical weapons either, leading to a very unnatural military situation. Had Hitler not had personal experience of the horrors of using gas on the battlefield, World War II would almost certainly have been conducted in a very different (and far more brutal) manner.

When Hitler heard news of the armistice, he reacted very bitterly, and looked to his own hatreds to provide answers. Although finding other people to blame was his way of dealing with his personal situation, he was far from alone, since the vast majority of the German people also wanted someone else to blame. From his distorted perspective, he could give them answers as to why they'd lost the war, why the economy had collapsed, and why the country was in political turmoil—the 'Great Jewish Conspiracy' had became his banner.

Hitler was a man of paradoxes—on the one hand he had shown himself to be lazy, arrogant and riddled with delusions of grandeur, but on the other hand he'd volunteered for military service, had been decorated for bravery, and never drank alcohol or smoked tobacco. On top of this he was a vegetarian who loved animals, and a hypochondriac who constantly worried about his health. In the post-Great War era, he found himself in the midst of all the political and economic uncertainty that was tearing Germany apart. It was into this climate of revolts, Putsch's and demonstrations that he now threw himself.

The Kapp Putsch was an unsuccessful military revolt against the Republican government that took place in mid March 1920—it was followed by several other uprisings by radical elements, however, all these also failed to take hold. The feelings of resentment amongst the German people were further stirred when Upper Silesia was partitioned from Germany and handed over to Poland in 1922. Although reparations payments were temporarily suspended due to the weakness of the economy, by January 1923 the Belgians and French felt that the Germans were dragging their heels over restarting the payments. In an attempt to encourage the appearance of more funds, Belgian and French were sent troops into the Ruhr. This created even more bad feeling in the local German population, and the combination of passive

Hitler enjoying a break while electioneering in the Harz mountains.

resistance and miner's strikes put the economy into meltdown.

Things were going from bad to worse for the German government—in October 1923, Bavaria and Rhineland both declared independence. Hitler felt the time was right to try and seize power, and launched the notorious Beer Hall Putsch in Munich—this attempted coup d'état failed miserably, and Hitler spent 12 months or so in prison. Meanwhile the economy continued to decline—inflation was so high that when devaluation took place, one new Mark was set at the equivalent of one trillion of the old ones. This completely wiped out the savings of Germany's middle and upper classes, something that once again fostered the feelings of anger and resentment. This left the door wide open for political opportunists to make trouble, especially those who could provide excuses to blame others, with the Jews being the favourite target for much of this black propaganda.

When Hitler was released from prison, he decided that he need some effective muscle if he was going to make his way in these troubled times. His solution was to start what was known as the *Sturm Abteilung* or SA, which translates as Storm Section. They were given uniforms with distinctive brown coloured shirts—rather unsurprisingly, they were soon nicknamed simply the 'brownshirts'. They performed two main functions—firstly to break up the meetings of Hitler's political opponents, and secondly to act as his bodyguard. Many of the recruits to this organisation had previously belonged to the Freikorps, and so were used to the idea of using violence for political ends.

One of the reason that Hitler attracted so much support in this period is that his book *Mein Kampf* was avidly read by vast numbers of German

The Obersalzberg in Bavaria was the location of Hitler's favourite hideaway—the Berghof. He first moved into a wooden farmhouse in 1925 but by the 1930s it had been completely rebuilt. These scenes show Hitler in casual clothing greeting locals, in conversation with Göring (below left) and talking to 'Ein Kamerad aus dem Feld'*—a fellow soldier from the first war.*

Hitler in the passenger seat of his Mercedes.

people. They lapped up suggestions that the German people was of superior stock, and that every cultural, artistic, scientific or technical advancement in human history was almost entirely due to the Aryan race's creative power.

His warnings that the Aryan strain was being polluted by intermarriage with barbarian blood stirred up ill-feeling towards the Jews and Slavs. He'd been blaming the Jews for Germany losing World War I ever since the conflict ended, and in *Mein Kampf* he claimed that they were trying to control the country by taking over the main political party, the German Social Democrat Party, along with many of the largest companies and several of the country's leading newspapers. Since the Jews owned a large number of the banks and money-lending organisations in Germany, a large proportion of the German population stood to gain financially if the Jews were dispossessed.

Hitler also declared that if he came to power, he would send military forces to occupy Russian land that would then act as a buffer zone for the defence of Germany as well as provide *Lebensraum*—living space—or the German people.

The situation in Germany was a great worry to the allies, who knew that instability could well lead to war once again. In order to try and kickstart the economy, the Dawes Plan was initiated in 1924—this reduced the reparations burden, and provided large American loans to German companies. Headed by Charles G. Dawes, the plan was initially successful—it slowed the rate of inflation, removed allied troops from the Ruhr, reorganised the German Reichsbank, and lowered the level of reparations for four years. While business started to recover, it soon became apparent that the high level of reparations was not economically sustainable. This provided further fuel for the likes of Hitler who complained that such plans did not lower the overall amount of reparations that Germany had to pay.

In 1925 Ebert died, and Field Marshal Paul von Hindenburg was elected as President of the Republic in his place. The next year Germany

Hitler's open-topped Mercedes.

was finally admitted to the League of Nations, which was a sign that it was at last being readmitted to the world stage. This was backed up by the Young Plan which replaced the Dawes Plan, and took effect in June 1929; it reduced the massive reparations payments that Germany was committed to. This was the allies way of recognising that the German economy could not possibly manage to meet its existing obligations and survive.

In the late 1920s Hitler predicted that economic disaster was on its way, but since things were better for the common people than they had been for years, his warnings were laughed at. However, just as it looked as though there was a way out of the gloom for Germany, out of the blue things went from bad to worse with the onset of the Wall Street Crash. This meant that all the American loans given out to German companies were suddenly recalled, which was an absolute disaster, not only for the nation but for the entire European economy. The unexpected downturn left many millions of people with what seemed to be a very bleak future. All of a sudden, Hitler's warnings seemed a lot more sensible than they had previously.

It was in times like these that extremist views tend to be more widely supported, and the Nazi Party was no exception. Vast numbers of people were left jobless as unemployment tripled when companies laid off workers or closed for business. Unemployment rose from 8.5 percent in 1929 to 14 percent in 1930, and then to 21.9 percent in 1931. At its peak it got as high as 29.9 percent in 1932. Hitler's message was popular—he claimed to have the answers that were needed to pull Germany out of economic depression, and the whole population understood that what was needed above all else was a strong leader. These factors combined to sway many voters in his direction, and Hitler did what he could to capitalise on them.

In March 1930, a new minority government was formed after the previous coalition collapsed—composed

Hitler flies to another rally.

On the Bückeberg during the 1934 Harvest Festival.

of elements from the right-wing and centre parties, it was led by Heinrich Brüning. This government had to rely on President von Hindenburg's emergency powers, and in an attempt to bolster his position, Brüning called a national election. The people, however, had been polarised by the prevailing economic uncertainty, and both the Nazis and the Communists polled large numbers of votes. During the course of 1931, the German financial situation just got worse and worse. At one stage the entire nation's banks had to close, and things got so bad that America, France and Britain had to give Germany a huge loan.

Since the Nazis were desperate to get their hands on political power, they decided that they should form their own intelligence and security organisation. This would give them access to information and secrets that could be used against their opponents, or indeed, against their own members, if need be. This unit was created by Heinrich Himmler in August 1931, and was called the SD or *Sicherheitsdienst.* Richard Heydrich was appointed as the head of the SD, and it was kept as a distinct unit from the uniformed Schutz Staffel (SS), who were Hitler's personal bodyguard.

Hitler and his entourage enjoyed flexing their muscles by sending the SA in to 'sort out' anyone who voiced alternative opinions to those held by the Nazis. As a result, the brownshirts gained a reputation for violence, and since they outnumbered the regular army by four to one, the Chancellor, Heinrich Brüning, feared that they would try to take over the country in a violent coup. In an attempt to allay such fears, he made the SA an illegal organisation.

Brüning's main intention was to get the allies to halt Germany's reparations payments by making such drastic budget cuts that the people's suffering would leave no other course of action open. While the ploy succeeded—US president Herbert Hoover finally declared a reparations moratorium in 1932, Brüning had made himself extremely unpopular with the people, and the country teetered on the edge of civil war.

By April 1932, the Nazis had so much popular support that Hitler only just lost out to Hindenburg in the presidential elections. Shortly after this Brüning, who had lost Hindenburg's confidence was replaced by Franz von Papen as German Chancellor. Papen was a member of the Catholic Centre Party, who were much more sympathetic to the views held by the Nazis than the SDP had been. In June, Papen's government lifted the ban on the SA or brownshirts, and to the great relief of the entire German people, the allies agreed to end Germany's reparations payments. On top of this, as a result of the latest national elections in July, the Nazis doubled their representation in the Reichstag, greatly improving their political influence.

Hindenburg and Hitler.

*Hitler speaks to new recruits of the Hitler Youth and League of German girls (*Bund Deutscher Mädel*) at the Hall of Heroes in Munich.*

Chancellor Papen did his best to tame Hitler by offering him the job of vice chancellor in his new cabinet, but Hitler was not interested in anything except the chancellorship. This signalled the start of a new phase in the nation's politics.

The presence of a large number of Communist representatives meant that it was not possible for the government to form a constructive coalition, so a further national election was held in November of 1932. This was inconclusive, so things did not get any better. Earlier in the same year Hitler had declared that he would not serve in the German government in any role other than as Chancellor, however, when a new one was appointed it was Major General Kurt von Schleicher who took the role, not Hitler. This infuriated Hitler, and within two months he had managed to convince enough prominent industrialists that a Communist revolution was underway—they in turn put Hindenburg under pressure to make Hitler the Chancellor in place of Schleicher.

Schleicher had been Papen's war minister, and as such was capable of handling the tough situation he could see before him. He realised that Hitler was prepared to use a violent overthrow of the standing government if necessary, and so he tried to convince President Hindenburg that the best course of action would be to dissolve the Reichstag and impose emergency powers. Hindenburg refused to take a part in such a policy, and in frustration Schleicher resigned.

Hitler knew that the time was right to start bombarding the people with propaganda, and so his master

Hitler speaking at Blohm & Voss.

Hitler at the Reichsführerschule*—a special school for training future Nazi leaders—at Bernau bei Berlin, just northeast of the capital.*

Hitler and Konstantin Hierl, the Secretary of State for Labour, in front of 47,000 workers of the Reichsarbeitdienst *(Reich Labour Service), Nuremberg 1935.*

Winston Churchill spoke out against appeasement of Nazi Germany during the 1930s.

manipulator Joseph Goebbels stepped into action. He instituted a media campaign that went for a blanket coverage of the Nazis main policies. While it was aimed at the disaffected unemployed, it was also designed to appeal to the large numbers of people whose standard of living had declined since the end of World War I. This included everything from farmers to white-collar workers, as well as young people who were attracted to Hitler's strong nationalist ideals.

Throughout this period, the allies had to juggle their priorities carefully. On the one hand they had their own domestic problems to deal with, and the last thing they wanted—or could afford, was to get involved in another conflict with Germany. On the other, they had to field claims of 'appeasement' from those who felt that the allies were being too lenient in their dealings with Hitler and his government. Chief amongst these characters was Winston Churchill, who did his best to alert the allies to the threat from Nazi Germany.

Both Britain and France were more or less bankrupted by World War I, and were still trying to recover financially. America had not been affected nearly as badly, but all the same had its hands full with the severe problems caused by the Great Depression. It is not surprising therefore that the allied politicians were doing all they could to deny that Germany posed any kind of military threat.

A further perspective that influenced the allied politicians' thinking was that the appalling conditions in the German domestic economy had generated quite a lot of sympathy around the world. This feeling fostered claims that war reparations had been set at too high a level, and many influential leaders thought that Germany should not have to continue paying up. This was especially true amongst those who were worried about the rise of communism—they felt that Germany was doing a good job of stemming the flow of revolutionary left-wing politics towards the west. As another war loomed, Hitler tested the water by watching the reactions of the allies to his actions in supporting the Spanish Civil War. They demonstrated a 'do nothing' policy, which was to have serious repercussions in the very near future.

NAZI GERMANY

Once he had achieved his aims of becoming chancellor, Hitler began to remove any sign of opposition from potential enemies. The Nazis had a word which described how they intended to go about this—*Gleichschaltung*, translates as consolidation or synchronisation. It was the establishment of a system that controlled and co-ordinated all aspects of society.

The starting point was the elimination of any non-Nazi organisations that could exert influence over the people—these included trade unions and political parties. Even the church did not escape this process—the Nazis established the Ministry of Ecclesiastical Affairs to ensure that no messages came across that could undermine Hitler's work.

When fire destroyed part of the Reichstag building at the end of February 1932, he used this as an excuse to go after many of his enemies. He forced President Hindenburg to issue the Reichstag Fire Decree. This put most human rights on hold, which allowed the Nazis to arrest any political adversaries—particularly the Communists, and also to let the SA loose to terrorise the voters in the upcoming elections. This wave of violence did not impress many of the German people, and to Hitler's immense annoyance, his party only polled 44percent of the vote. This was not enough to claim a clear majority, so the Nazis started removing the remaining Communist members either by arresting them on spurious charges, or by terrorising them so that they went underground. It was not long before the

Hitler meeting and greeting during a journey through East Prussia.

Delegation from the Saar in front of the Chancellery, Berlin.

Nazis had eradicated enough of their opposition to rule without hindrance.

In order to give themselves even greater powers, the Enabling Act was passed—this transferred all legislative powers to Hitler's government, which removed the requirement for the Reichstag to approve any legislation passed by the cabinet. It effectively abolished the remainder of the Weimar constitution. With this procedure taken care of, the Nazis banned the Communist and Social Democratic parties. The Third Reich had now legitimised itself, and would prove to be unstoppable by anything except military means.

The new government wasted little time in consolidating their bigotries and removing any possible opponents. In April 1933, the 'Law for the Restoration of the Professional Civil Service' started a purge from the service of all Jews, Communists and other people considered to be any kind of a threat to the regime. This was backed up a month later by making the Nazis the only legal political party—all the others were closed down.

In order to stimulate the economy, the Nazis instituted the first Reinhardt Plan—this was a massive attempt to reduce unemployment and return the country to prosperity through government spending. The money—one billion Reichsmarks, was spent in two major ways; one of these was on large-scale public works such as housing, motorways and bridges. The other was on rearmament—many of the unemployed were absorbed into the army, and huge sums were spent on military equipment. A second Reinhardt Plan added another half billion Reichsmarks later the same year.

While the plans succeeded in increasing the country's prosperity, many of the methods used to raise the money were not sustainable—the government printed large amounts of extra currency, and used highly dubious financing deals to create new armaments companies. In order to hide the scale of rearmament, the

Like all political leaders before and since, Hitler spent much time courting the popular vote through walkabouts and visits to hospitals, etc.

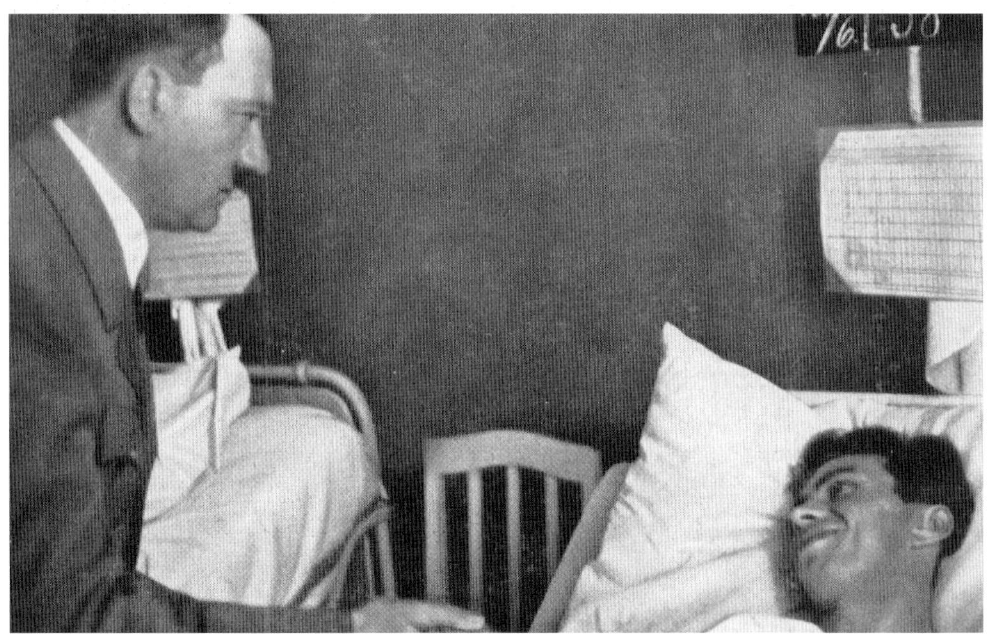

government stopped the publication of data concerning the national budget in 1934. To the great concern of the allies, not only was Germany in the process of rearming, it also withdrew from the Disarmament Conference and the League of Nations. Conscious of these feelings, Hitler tried to convince the world that he only had peaceful intentions, and signed a non-aggression treaty with Poland. This was a two-edged sword—not only did it serve to allay fears of future German aggression, it also undermined attempts by the allies to build up military alliances and defences.

At this time Hitler also had some significant domestic problems to deal with. Although the SA had been legitimised by Papen's government in June 1932, their time had come. Until then Hitler had manipulated them to his own ends, using the band of thugs to murder, terrorise and threaten anyone who stood in the way of the Nazi Party. The leader of the SA, Ernst Röhm had ambitions that threatened Hitler—he wanted, for instance, to overthrow the regular army so that the SA could become the dominant military force. It certainly was large enough—while the regular army numbered only 100,000 (the maximum it was allowed under the Treaty of Versailles), the SA numbered more than 400,000. This idea did not fit in with Hitler's master plan, however, and with the encouragement of Herman Göring (who commanded the Prussian Gestapo and was Röhm's arch rival), he ordered the Himmler's SS to massacre the leaders of the SA—including Röhm, who was on old friend of Hitler's. This infamous event became known as the Night of the Long Knives.

With the SA out of the way, Himmler reorganised the SS to turn it into one of the largest and most powerful organisations in Germany. To do this he knew that his recruits would have to be well-disciplined and fanatically loyal, unlike the drunken thugs of the SA. To attract the best people, Himmler created an elitist image by the use of distinct black uniforms and special insignia. Himmler made the SS swear allegiance to Adolf Hitler, with the motto *My honour is loyalty*—this was a clever move, since it made Hitler feel comfortable that the SS existed with the aim of furthering

Another huge rally greets their leader.

The Reichstag—the German parliament—burns on the night of February 27, 1933. From its ashes would rise Hitler's Third Reich.

his ambitions, and no-one else's. It gave Himmler an enormous amount of power, and the SS became the backbone of the Nazi party.

The racial purity card was something that the Nazis had been playing since the early 1930's, and Himmler was responsible for implementing many of the relevant policies. In 1931 he formed the Race and Resettlement Central Office, which was also known as 'RUSHA'—its purpose was check to that all SS men were racially pure, since Himmler believed that his men were the basis of a new Nordic master race. All new SS recruits had to show paper records proving that they had no Jewish, Slavic, or other 'undesirable' blood lines as far back as 1750. This also included checks to ensure that they had no genetic medical issues or mental health problems. Since the idea was to create a new race composed entirely of pure Aryan children, any prospective SS wives also had to go through the same checking procedures.

In August 1934, President von Hindenburg died—this gave Hitler the chance to assume the Presidency as well as the Chancellorship. In order to legitimise the move, he organised a national vote, but in doing so he also ensured that no-one was able to voice any public disapproval of the idea. With no contrary messages to consider, the German public supported Hitler with 88percent of the vote in his favour. In order to form a successful government, the Nazis created an alliance with the conservatives—in the short-term, this suited Hitler's agenda, but their period of usefulness would prove to be short-lived.

Hitler speaking at Nuremberg.

In 1934, Hitler's cabinet was composed of the following members:

Position	Position (translated)	Name	Years in Office
Führer und Reichskanzler	Führer & Chancellor	Adolf Hitler	1934–1945
Reichsarbeitsminister	Minister of Labour	Franz Seldte	1933–1945
Reichsaußenminister	Minister for Foreign Affairs	Konstantin von Neurath	1932–1938
Reichsfinanzminister	Minister of Finances	Lutz Schwerin von Krosigk	1933–1945
Reichsjustizminister	Minister of Justice	Franz Gürtner	1933–1941
Reichsminister des Innern	Minister of Interior	Wilhelm Frick	1933–1943
Reichsminister für Ernährung und Landwirtschaft	Minister of Agriculture	Walther Darré	1933–1943
Reichsminister für Luftfahrt	Minister of Air	Hermann Göring	1933–1945
Reichsminister für Volksaufklärung und Propaganda	Minister for Public Enlightenment and Propaganda	Joseph Goebbels	1933–1945
Reichsminister für Wissenschaft, Erziehung und Volksbildung	Minister for Science, Education and Culture	Bernhard Rust	1934–1945
Reichsverkehrs- und Reichspostminister	Minister of Post and Communication	Paul Freiherr von Eltz-Rübenach	1933–1937
Reichswehrminister	Minister of Defence	Werner von Blomberg	1933–1938
Reichswirtschaftsminister	Minister of Economics	Hjalmar Schacht	1933–1937

Hitler and Hjalmar Schacht at the laying of the foundation stone for the new Reichsbank, May 5, 1934. Schacht was Minister of Economics 1933–37.

Hitler and his cabinet.

Hitler at a motor show in Berlin, 1935.

Hitler greeted by his adoring countrymen, Bückeberg 1935.

Hitler applauds Wilhelm Furtwängler, the conductor of the Berlin Philharmonic Orchestra.

Above: Hjalmar Schacht resigned as Minister of Economics in 1937 and as Reichsbank President in 1939. Imprisoned after the July Bomb Plot he was lucky to survive the war. On trial at Nuremberg, he was found not guilty of war crimes.

With the matter of political control out of the way, Hitler became a lot more brazen in his actions. In 1935 he disregarded the disarmament clauses of the Versailles Treaty and stepped up the process of rearmament. The allies could see that Germany was growing powerful once again, and Britain's politicians tried to deal with this by signing various accords with her. This was labelled as 'appeasement' by those who were opposed to standing by and allowing Germany to rearm. Foremost among such people were politicians like Winston Churchill, who mistrusted Hitler from the start.

A further tightening of the Nazis grip on power occurred in June 1936 when Himmler was appointed to the position of Chief of the German Police—he then divided the system into two distinct divisions. The first was called the *Ordungspolizei*, and was made up of regular uniformed police, whilst the second—and more sinister section, was called the *Sicherheitspolizei*, or Security police. This unit included the Gestapo, and was run by Himmler's number two—the brutal Reinhard Heydrich.

In 1936 the Nazis stepped up pressure on the Jews by enacting the Nuremberg Laws which deprived them of their citizenship rights. For many people of Jewish origin this was the last straw, and large numbers of them left the country to seek friendlier climes. If this wasn't enough to alert the allies to Hitler's true intentions, he then sent troops into the demilitarised Rhineland in clear violation of the Versailles and Locarno Treaties.

When Germany annexed Austria in spring 1938, the Nazis began systematically expelling the large

Below: Hitler lays the foundations of the meeting house in the Adolf-Hitler-Koog, reclaimed land in Dithmarschen on the North Sea coast of Schleswig-Holstein.

Above: Hitler greets youthful workers at the Chancellery on May 1, 1934, National Labour Day.

numbers of Jews from the country. Although the rich could afford to pay for travel to friendlier shores, the poorer elements could not. In order to organise their expulsion, the Nazis set up the 'Central Office of Jewish Emigration' in Vienna. This was run by Adolf Eichmann, who ran the system there very smoothly and efficiently—he was known to his peers as the 'Jewish Specialist'. He extorted large sums of money from the richer members of the Jewish community to pay for exit visas for the poor. Within 18 months, he had reduced the Jewish population in Austria by half. Eichmann's example was extremely highly regarded within the Nazi party, and it was not long before 'Offices of Jewish Emigration' were established throughout the German Reich.

Below: Hitler and Dr. Robert Ley, head of the German Labour Front, during the 1935 Nuremberg Rally.

The Nazis hatred of the Jews continued to build, and in late 1938,

Hitler loved architecture: here he is seen with Professors Troost and Wackerle studying a model in Munich.

Adoring crowds greet Hitler as he leaves the House of German Art in Munich.

Hitler acknowledges the crowd during the Bayreuth festival.

And this is the Bayreuth crowd!

Another view of Hitler at the 1935 Berlin Motor Show.

Hitler talks to workers at the Adolf-Hitler-Koog.

things got a lot worse after what is known as the 'Night of broken glass', or *Kristallnacht*. This marked the start of a campaign of violent persecution—synagogues and other Jewish properties were burnt, and thousands of Jews were beaten up and arrested.

Education

A major part of the success of the Nazi party must be attributed to the manner in which they indoctrinated their youth through a targeted education system. Hitler was under no illusions as to the usefulness of intellectual subjects. He stated that: 'Knowledge is ruin to my young men. A violent, active, dominating, brutal youth—that is what I am after.' He also said that, 'The German youth of the future must be swift like the greyhound,

Hitler on a factory visit receives the "German Greeting".

tough like leather, and hard like Krupp steel.' In order to achieve this, an education system was established that ensured that Germany's young minds were filled with propaganda driven ideals of honour and patriotism for the Fatherland.

The Nazis forced all Germany's teachers to join the National Socialist Teachers League, and in doing so and they had to swear an oath to 'be loyal and obedient to Adolf Hitler'. No Jewish teachers were allowed to keep their posts, and if there was any doubt about their loyalty they were dismissed. Special schools were set up for Jewish children, who were no longer allowed to attend mainstream German schools. The racial divide was further enforced with the inclusion of 'Racial Sciences' into the school curriculum. This was designed to indoctrinate children into the idea that the German people were genetically superior to Jewish and others of mixed blood. This concept was extended right across the board of educational subjects—history lessons were changed to lectures on Hitler's life, and in maths lessons instead of counting oranges and apples, examples were based on bombs and craters.

Manipulating the minds of children while they were at school wasn't enough for Hitler though. He wanted to toughen them up physically as well—and felt they should join militarised youth organisations. As a result the *Hitlerjugend*, or Hitler Youth was formed in June 1933—this was run by Baldur von Schirach, who made it into one of the largest groups of its kind in the world. Based on existing youth

Hitler visits the Bavarian State Library.

Hitler at shipbuilders Blohm & Voss.

Hitler greeted by German girls.

The opening of the autobahn between Frankfurt and Darmstadt in 1935. From left to right: von Blomberg (Minister of Defence), Hitler, Dr. Todt (head of Organisation Todt, the unit set up in 1938 to build military installations and autobahns suitable for military use), Dr. Schacht (president of Reichsbank), Dr. Dorpmüller (director of German railways), Goebbels.

Hitler looks over the Rhine at Bad Godesberg on September 24, 1938, during the negotiations with Neville Chamberlain over Czechoslovakia.

Hitlerjugend drummers at the 1935 Nuremberg Rally: 54,000 youths attended.

groups, it focused on physical activities such as sports and living rough in the outdoors, with camping and hiking trips being especially favoured. The organisation differed from the others in that if featured lectures on patriotism and taught boys how to become fighters.

Breeding Racial Purity

Since the Nazis believed they were starting a 'Thousand Year Reich', they wanted to ensure a plentiful supply of racially pure 'Nordic' children. Himmler was particularly preoccupied with this, and told his SS men that they should, 'Show that you are ready, through your faith in the Führer and for the sake of the life of our blood and people, to regenerate life for Germany just as bravely as you know how to fight and die for Germany.' He told them that they should have at least four children, and that they should not only make their wives pregnant, but any other 'racially pure' women as well—this would not be adultery as it was in the nation's best interests.

The concept was carried forward in other ways as well—special maternity units were set up for unmarried mothers to give birth. Called 'Spring of Life' (*Lebensborn*) homes, generally were places that had been confiscated from wealthy Jews. Those women who did not want to keep their babies were able to have them adopted by SS families, and special accolades were given to mothers who produced four or more children.

Racial Cleansing

In stark contrast to Himmler's interest in the fostering of German babies, he ordered his SS men to commit acts of barbarism on those he considered to be 'subhuman' in a reign of terror throughout the occupied territories. Anyone though to be Jewish, Slavic or communist was seen as an enemy, and therefore fair game to SS brutality.

The allies were well aware of what was going on, and in 1940 Clement Attlee gave a speech in the House of Commons, in which he said, '*We are now faced with the danger of the world relapsing into barbarism. Nazism is the outstanding menace to civilisation, not only because of the character and actions of the men who are in absolute control of a great nation, but because of their ideas which are openly in conflict with all the conceptions upon which civilised life is based.*'

Electioneering in 1932.

All children joined either the Hitlerjugend *or* Bund Deutscher Mädel *when they reached the age of 14/15—so long as their ancestry was "pure".*

In 1941, Hitler ordered the physical extermination of the Jews—this was to be called the *Endlösung*—the Final Solution. Heydrich and Eichmann were tasked with implementing this new wave of atrocities. Instead of permitting Jews to emigrate, they were to be shipped to concentration camps where they would be killed in special killing centres. These were to be well away from the scrutiny of the western world, hidden in the depths of the eastern Germany Reich. Eichmann would take control of transporting the Jews to the camps, and would co-ordinate the capabilities of each killing centre to optimise their efficiency.

One of the problems that such a plan posed was just how they would kill such large numbers of people quickly and cheaply. Eichmann discussed this with Rudolf Hoss, the commandant

Hitler makes his mark—1: Munich's Königsplatz after rebuilding.

Hitler makes his mark—2: The colonnaded House of German Art in Munich.

Hitler makes his mark—3: Model of a projected congress hall in Nuremberg.

Summer 1935, Hitler surveys the bridge carrying the Munich-Salzburg autobahn over the Mangfall valley in Bavaria.

Above and Below: Hitler greets children at Obersalzberg.

of Auschwitz, which was the largest of the concentration camps. Together they decided that a potassium cyanide gas that was widely used as a rat poison called 'Zyklon B' was the most suitable agent.

The Final Solution needed the complicity of many leading Nazis, and to ensure that they all toed the line, Reinhard Heydrich and Adolf Eichmann organised the Wannsee Conference in 1942. Wannsee was a plush suburb of Berlin, and was a most unlikely setting for a meeting that was intended to co-ordinate the killing of 11 million innocent people. It was entitled the 'Final Solution to

caption

Hitlerjugend march past the Brown House in Munich, the headquarters of the leadership of the NSDAP from 1931.

the Jewish Question', and it gained the support of all those who attended.

Knowing he had unquestioning support, Eichmann methodically organised just how he was going to move so many people out of their homes and move them across large distances to the various concentration camps. Officially they were told that they were being resettled in the east—this was not only to keep them from panicking and trying to escape, but it also ensured the support of the common German people. Fake propaganda films were made showing the Jews being moved into comfortable homes and enjoying their new lifestyle, and so little resistance was felt.

The ethnic cleansing was done in a rigorous 'area by area' manner, with the Jews being told to take their belongings and wait at predetermined locations to join a train. Once there, they were put into over-crowded boxcars, with no food, water or toilets. If this was not bad enough, the trains did not stop for several days, and large numbers of people died from starvation,

Another photo opportunity.

Hitler talks to workmen building a motorway.

Opening of the first stretch of the Munich–Salzburg autobahn.

Aerial view. The motorways helped put men back to work and did much to solidify the economy.

Hitler takes the salute from his car during the 1934 Nuremberg Rally.

dehydration and illness. Eichmann was responsible for the transportation a many millions of people—these included not just Jews, but also Poles, Czechs, Russians, gypsies, communists and other 'undesirables'. Even though the vast majority of these people died in the killing centres, after the war had ended Eichmann refused to take any responsibility, saying that he was just 'obeying orders' from his superiors.

A large number of those shipped to the concentration camps were used as slave labour—this could be anything from work in armaments factories to mining—it could even be involved in running the killing 'ovens' where countless numbers of people lost their lives. Conditions were so bad for the slave workers that huge numbers of them died from malnutrition, exhaustion and disease. Others were executed for the slightest infringement of camp rules. The factories that used these workers made complaints to Himmler that the workers were dying faster than they could be replaced, and in the interests of German armaments production, conditions were improved enough to reduce the death rate. Himmler himself stated that:

'What happens to a Russian, to a Czech, does not interest me in the slightest... Whether nations live in prosperity or starve to death like cattle interests me only in so far as we need them as slaves to our culture; otherwise it is of no interest to me. Whether 10,000 Russian females fall down from exhaustion while digging an antitank ditch interests me only in so far as the antitank ditch for Germany is finished.'

Hitler at the 1935 Nuremberg Rally. In the car with him are Hess and von Schirach.

Himmler's stated lack of concern for the fate of slave labourers was not merely verbal—a witness who saw conditions at the Krupp Works which produced armaments said that:

'The clothing of the Eastern workers was likewise completely inadequate. They worked and slept in the same clothing in which they had arrived from the East. Virtually all of them had no overcoats and were compelled to use their blankets as coats in the cold and rainy weather. In view of the shortage of shoes many workers were forced to go to work in their bare feet even in winter... The sanitary conditions were atrocious. At Kramerplatz only ten children's toilets were available for 1,200 inhabitants... The Tartars and Kirghiz suffered the most; they collapsed like flies from bad housing, insufficient food, overwork, and insufficient rest. These workers were likewise afflicted with spotted fever. Lice, the carrier of the disease, together with the countless fleas, bugs and other vermin tortured the inhabitants of these camps.'

While conditions were improved enough to maintain the supply of workers needed to keep the munitions factories open, the casualty figures were still appalling. Deaths occurred from malnutrition, disease and beatings right up to the end of the war. Even then, the toll still continued as a result of injuries sicknesses, and of those who survived, many were so traumatised by their experiences that they never fully recovered.

The Day of National Mourning, March 16, 1934.

Harvest Festival 1934: Hitler at the Goslar Imperial Palace.

State governors meet in Berlin.

Hitler meets a Japanese naval delegation, 1934.

Foreign military attachés salute the march past at a Nuremberg Rally.

Labour Day, May 1, 1934.

1936 Olympic Games

The eleventh Olympic Games took place in Berlin in 1936 and gave the Nazis a heaven-sent opportunity (they were awarded before the Nazis came to power) to show off their organisational skills—as well as showing the world that Germany was a phoenix risen from the ashes of Versailles. Anti-Jewish fervour was put on hold for the games; great new stadia were constructed; huge pageants were prepared.

Hitler was not disappointed on the first day: Hans Woellke won the shot-putt gold medal, Germany's first ever field gold and Tilly Fleischer the javelin gold. However, without doubt the hero of the games was the black American Jesse Owens with four golds (100m, Long jump, 200m and 400m relay). Hitler—whose view was that blacks, like Jews, were racially inferior—absented himself from the medals ceremonies.

Leni Riefenstahl—director of Triumph of the Will, the propaganda film of the 1934 Nuremberg Rally—produced two prize-winning films of the Olympiad.

The Olympic Torch on its way to the stadium.

August 1, 1936: a parade of German youth in Berlin to watch the Olympic Torch arrive.

Hitler at the 1936 Winter Olympics held at Garmisch–Partenkirchen.

Hitler at the opening ceremony of the summer games.

Tilly Fleischer. Germany's gold medallist in the women's javelin.

Nazi salutes were de rigeur at the medal ceremonies.

Hitler and the Olympic Committee enter the stadium.

The quickest pair in the world—Jesse Owens and Helen Stephens.

Aerial view of the main stadium and the swimming pool.

Göring watches the ice hockey.

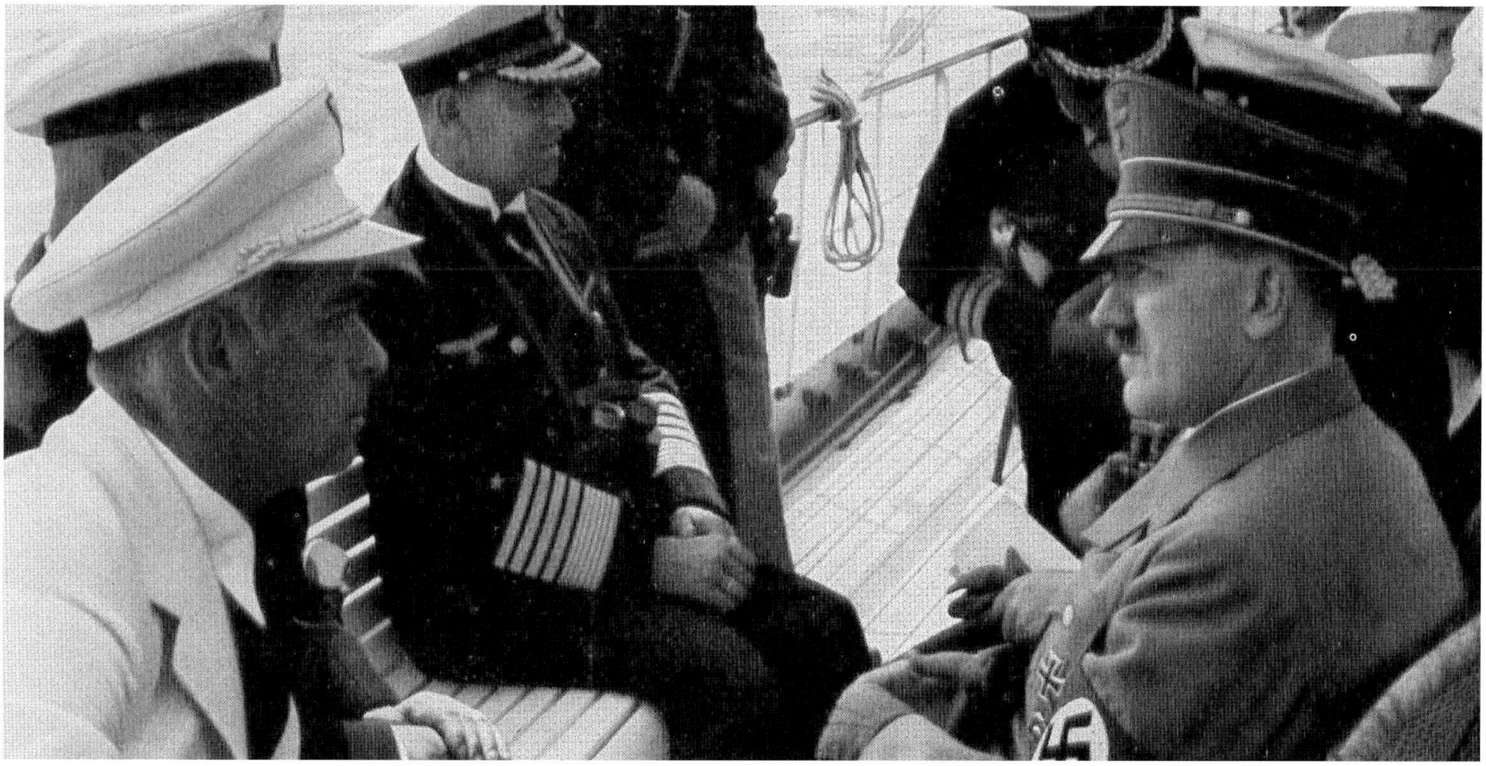

Hitler at the sailing confers with navy officials.

The Top Nazis

Adolf Hitler

It has been claimed that Adolf Hitler's deranged character was the product of his upbringing—he had an overly strict father to whom physical beatings were simply how you disciplined an unruly child. Hitler's mother tried to compensate for this by being overly affectionate, and when she died, he was absolutely devastated. He became fixated with anti-Semitism before the start of World War I, and when Germany lost, he—like many others, blamed the Jews. By using this as his rallying cry, he built up a large following, and he soon proved to be a hypnotic public speaker. He also gained popular approval by claiming that the Versailles Treaty should be rescinded, that war profits should be confiscated and that the Jews should lose their civil rights. On top of this he wanted recent Jewish immigrants to be expelled, and stirred up further hatred by claiming that the dire state of the economy was their fault

Throughout the early 1920s Hitler exploited public resentment at Germany's treatment at the hands of the Allies, and built up the Nazi Party with illegal mass protest rallies until it became a strong political force. Hitler then over-stepped the mark by attempting to stage a coup—this was known as the 'Beer Hall Putsch', and its failure resulted in him spending a year in prison. While he was locked away, he wrote *Mein Kampf*, where he presented his ideas on the future of the German peoples—and in particular how the Communists were in league with the Jews in an international conspiracy.

He reserved his real fury for his

Hitler was a remarkable orator who mesmerised his audience both with his rhetoric and his charismatic presence.

Hitler with Helga Goebbels.

Hitler and Goebbels—who would remain together until the end, the latter dying with his entire family in the Berlin bunker.

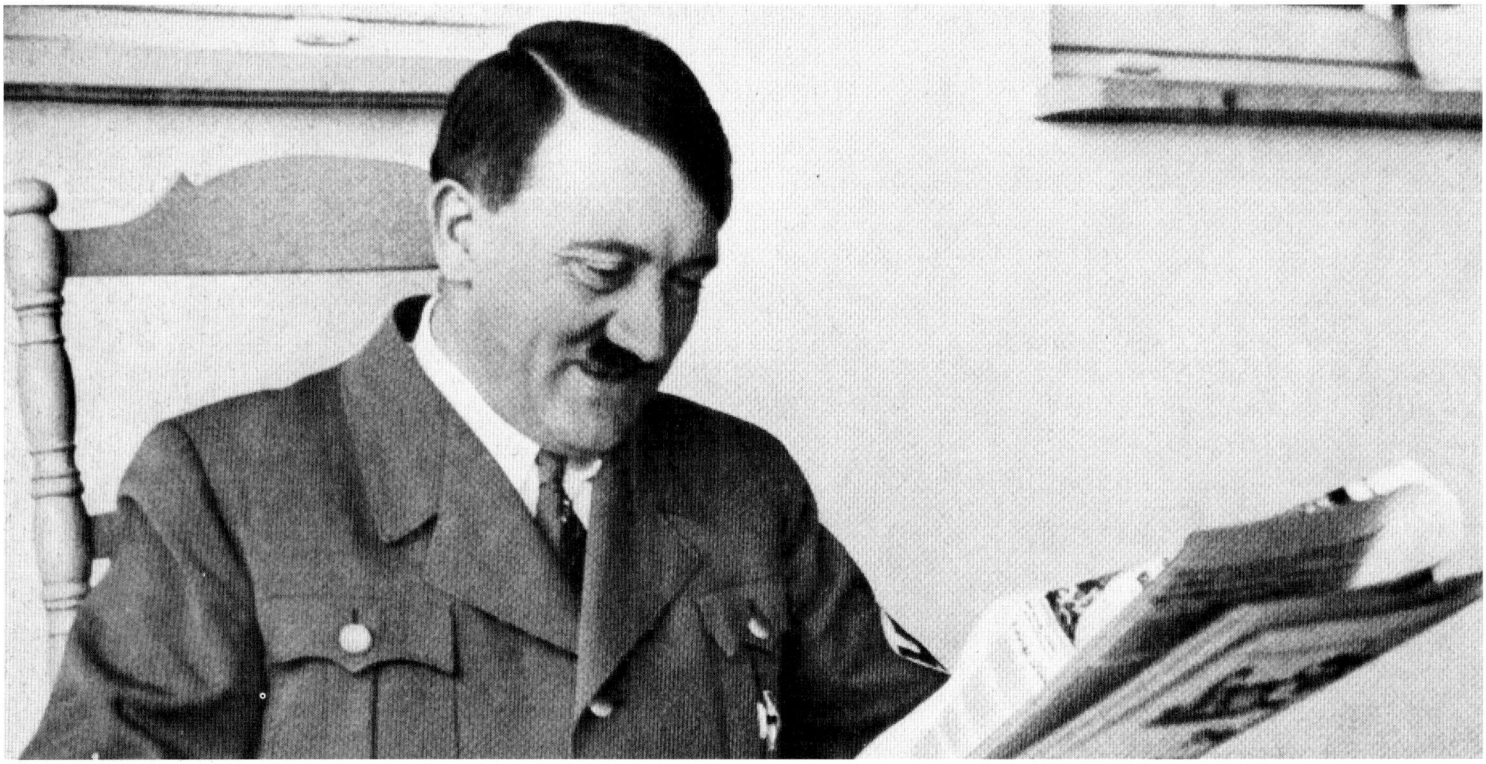

Hitler was much-photographed, particularly by Heinrich Hoffmann, whose photographic assistant, Eva Braun, would eventually become Hitler's wife.

A moody photograph of Hitler sitting beside the Obersee in Berchtesgaden.

Paul von Hindenburg died on August 2, 1934, and was buried in the Marshal's Tower at Tannenberg—the scene of his great victory against the Russians during World War I.

claims that the Jews were an anti-race hell-bent on the perversion of true German blood—specifically he said that they wanted 'the promiscuous bastardisation of other peoples'. The only way to stop them was to eliminate them, and by taking over their lands, the Germans would gain badly needed *Lebensraum*—living space. This was a particularly popular message with the vast numbers of people who were suffering in the overwhelming financial crisis the country was experiencing.

Hitler continued to gather support until he was made chancellor in 1933. From this point on he continued to strengthen his position by the use of murder, intimidation, deceit and intrigue. By the late 1930's he had built up the German economy by putting the entire country on a war footing. He ordered his armed forces to annex Austria and the Sudetenland in 1938, and then invaded Poland on September 1, 1939.

Hitler on his 47th birthday, April 20, 1936.

Such military action forced France and England to declare war on Germany, but this did not deter Hitler from going on to take most of Western Europe by using *Blitzkrieg* (lightning war) tactics. He then went on to invade the Soviet Union in August 1939, but early successes were reversed when the Russian winter took its toll on German forces, in particular with defeats at Moscow in December 1941 and Stalingrad through the winter of 1942-43. This coincided with America entering the war following the Japanese attack on Pearl Harbour, and was followed by total defeat in North Africa. This led to the Allies invasion of Italy and ultimately the re-taking of France in 1944. During this period the combined allied air forces destroyed most of Germany's industrial capacity and many of her towns and cities .

Despite many attempts on his life, Adolf Hitler survived until the Red Army entered Berlin. On April 30, 1945, when it was clear that all was lost, he married his mistress in a last-minute ceremony and then shot himself. He left behind him a Europe devastated by years of war, terror campaigns and racial cleansing.

Left: The Leibstandarte Adolf Hitler was the Führer's personal bodyguard that threw a cordon around him at the Nuremberg Rallies. It grew from the Stabswache Berlin into—by the end of World War II—the 1st SS-Panzer Division. The photo above shows Leibstandarte troops in Munich in 1935. The lower, a barracks inspection by Hitler and Leibstandarte commander Sepp Dietrich.

Above: Sepp Dietrich accompanies Hitler in a Leibstandarte inspection.

Below: A Leibstandarte soldier holds the 1923 Blutfahne *(Blood Banner) while Hitler takes the salute at a Nuremberg Rally march-past.*

Herman Göring

Herman Göring remains one of the better known characters of the Third Reich; he was born into the German aristocracy in Rosenheim, Bavaria on January 12, 1893. His father was a senior army officer, so it was natural for him to be educated at a military school. At the age of 19 he joined the German Army, and when World War I began he served with the infantry until rheumatoid arthritis of the knees hospitalised him. After this he joined the German Army Air Service, where he gained a reputation as an ace fighter pilot, with recorded 22 kills.

After the war, Göring became a civilian pilot, and went on to join the Nazi Party in 1922. As an open admirer of Hitler's, he soon became a leader of the Sturm Abteilung's brownshirts. His social status proved very useful to Hitler, since he had family contacts amongst Germany's leading industrialists. As a result of this, the Nazis were able to persuade many of these influential movers and shakers that the threat from the Bolsheviks was so great that the only way to prevent a collapse into Communism was to support the Nazis.

Göring played a small part in the infamous Beer Hall Putsch, but as a result of the medical treatment he was given for shrapnel wounds, he became addicted to morphine. While this did not significantly impair him for many years, later in his life he completely lost control of the addiction. Since the putsch had failed, those who took part were wanted criminals, and Göring was no exception. He fled to Sweden, where he stayed for four years—during this time his health declined and his weight increased dramatically; on his return to Germany he weighed 280lb.

Göring as commander-in-chief of the SA. He is wearing an Ehrhardt Brigade helmet and the Blue Max he won during World War I.

Göring's family connections undoubtedly helped him receive an amnesty from President Paul von Hindenburg in 1927, whereupon he returned to Berlin. Within a year he had been elected to the Reichstag as one of 12 Nazi Party members, and in August 1932 he was made President of the Nazi Party. When he became Chancellor, Hitler made Göring a cabinet minister without portfolio, and then not long after, minister of the interior and prime minister of Prussia. This post included control of the Geheime Staats Polizei (GESTAPO), and Göring wasted no time in ensuring the loyalty of these forces by replacing 22 of the 32 chief officers with members of the SA and SS.

Göring was instrumental in terrorising Hitler's political opponents, and together with Himmler and Heydrich organised the massacre of the SA's leaders in the Night of the Long Knives. After relinquishing control of the Gestapo to Himmler, Göring became head of the German Air Force—the Luftwaffe. At this time it had little military significance, since it was composed of small numbers of trainers and a few prototype aircraft. Göring was responsible for the utter transformation of the Luftwaffe into the most modern and powerful air force in the world.

Incredibly, Göring also oversaw the restructuring of the German economy into a system that was able to afford to rearm all three services (army, navy and air force), as well as create enough prosperity to maintain public morale. Hitler was so impressed by these achievements that he named Göring as his successor in 1939, and in 1940 appointed him to be Reichsmarschall.

Göring later in the war.

All this power and glory turned Göring into an arrogant and greedy man. He made vast fortunes from his activities, which included ownership of the *Essener National* newspaper. When war broke out in the summer of 1940, he further increased his standing by claiming responsibility for the rapid defeats of France, Netherlands, Belgium and Luxembourg. This did not last, however, and he lost credibility by putting too much faith in air power, a problem that was exacerbated by his boastful nature. As a result of this, he made many mistakes in how the Luftwaffe were used, and Hitler began to lose faith in him. This situation became much worse when, in contrast to his over-ambitious claims, the Luftwaffe failed to supply the German Sixth Army when they were under winter siege at Stalingrad. Hitler never forgave Göring, and blamed him for all manner of other military problems.

Since he had lost Hitler's respect, Göring spent much of the rest of the war plundering the museums and private homes of occupied Europe for art treasures for his own collections. During this time his morphine addiction got much worse, and began to lose contact with reality. When Berlin was surrounded by the Red Army, Hitler's communication lines were cut off, and Göring tried to implement earlier plans for him to assume command. Hitler considered this to be an overthrow, and had Göring arrested and replaced by Admiral Doenitz.

With the Red Army approaching, Göring surrendered to the US Army in Austria on 8th May, 1945. As a leader of the Nazi regime, he was later put on trial at Nuremberg for War Crimes and involvement in Crimes Against Humanity. He was found guilty, but before the sentence could be carried out, he committed suicide by swallowing a cyanide capsule on October 15, 1946.

Heinrich Himmler

After Adolf Hitler, the image of Heinrich Himmler probably represents the persona of the Third Reich more than any other. During his reign of terror he became one of the most powerful people in the world, and was directly responsible for the deaths of many millions of innocent civilians. He was described as 'the most unscrupulous figure in the Third Reich', and even Heydrich called him a sadist.

Heinrich Himmler was born in Munich on October 7, 1900, into a strict catholic middle class family. His father was a headmaster who had personally tutored the children of many influential families. As a result of these close ties, Prince Heinrich of Bavaria had agreed to become Himmler's godfather.

Although he was too young to join up for military service during World War I, Himmler played his part by joining an officer cadet unit. His main interests lay in agriculture, and so it was in this direction that he started training after leaving school. He worked on a farm for a while, and then went to Munich University as an agricultural student. After this he started to take an interest in politics—he worked as a technical assistant at a fertiliser company for a while, but then got increasingly involved in the Reichskriegsflagge, a paramilitary group led by Ernst Röhm. He also joined the Nazi Party, and was present at the Beer Hall Putsch, but took no significant part in what happened there.

When Hitler was jailed for leading the failed coup, the party's number two man, Gregor Strasser took control of the northern faction of the party. Himmler was hired by Strasser as his general assistant, which mostly involved keeping the office running and spreading propaganda. Himmler's logistical skills showed through very quickly, and before long he was put in charge of organising the SS in southern Bavaria. He continued to work his way upwards within the party, and in 1926, when Strasser was made party propaganda chief, Himmler moved with him to Munich as his deputy.

Heinrich Himmler, Reichsführer of the SS and leader of the Gestapo.

Himmler's fortunes improved further when Hitler appointed him to be National Commander (Reichsführer) of the SS in January 1929, and was especially pleased when the SS was made fully independent of the SA in 1931. Not long after this though, he started to see the SA as rivals to his SS, and together with Göring managed to convince Hitler that Rohm was plotting his overthrow. The result was the 'Night of the Long Knives', when the SS massacred the SA's higher echelons. After setting up the Race and Resettlement Central Office (RUSHA), he spent a lot of time trying to promote the idea of the Nordic race as superior beings.

In June 1936 Himmler became Chief of the German Police, which further increased his power and influence. He kept building up the SS, by the time war was approaching it had been split into two separate divisions, with one being military (the Waffen-SS) and the other non-military (the Allgemeine-SS). As war broke out, the Waffen SS were used to perform the most brutal atrocities, such as mass executions in civilian settlements, since most of the regular

German Army would not stand for such behaviour. The SS were also heavily involved in setting up and running the concentration camps, as well as being responsible for the mass killings of their inmates. On top of this, the SS did much of the organisation for the provision of slave labourers for the German war effort.

Himmler was dedicated to purging Germany of all but the purest genetic stock—in an address to his SS leaders, he stated that:

'It is not only the struggle of the nations, which in this case are put forward by the opposing side merely as a front, but it is the ideological struggle of the entire Jewry, freemasonry, Marxism, and churches of the world. These forces—of which I presume the Jews to be the driving spirit, the origin of all the negatives—are clear that if Germany and Italy are not annihilated, they will be annihilated. That is a simple conclusion. In Germany the Jew cannot hold out. This is a question of years. We will drive them out more and more with an unprecedented ruthlessness.'

Through the early stages of the war, Himmler carried on ordering and co-ordinating the deaths of millions of innocent people; Hitler was so pleased with his performance that in 1943 he also made him Minister of the Interior. As the war continued, however, Himmler realised that the Nazis could not win, and he began to negotiate with the Allies behind Hitler's back. He also realised that he could use the large numbers of concentration camp prisoners under his control as pawns in order to broker the best possible deal. This was in spite of the order given by Hitler that none should be allowed to fall into the hands of the Allies.

Himmler and Hitler watch German troop exercises.

As the war drew to a close, it became obvious that the Soviets were going to engulf vast areas as they marched on Berlin. The thought of being captured by the Red Army terrified everyone, junior and senior officers and men alike, and Himmler was no exception. He tried to get the Allies to accept the Nazi's surrender, on the condition that they then joined forces to defeat the Soviets. When Hitler got word that Himmler was talking to the Allies behind his back, he took it as the worst act of treachery that he had ever known. In his will, Hitler wrote:

'Before my death, I expel the former Reichsführer of the SS and Minister of the Interior Heinrich Himmler from the party and from all his state offices. Apart altogether from their disloyalty to me, Göring and Himmler have brought irreparable shame on the whole nation by secretly negotiating with the enemy without my knowledge and against my will, and also by illegally attempting to seize control of the State.'

After the fall of the Third Reich, Himmler attempted to evade the Allies with disguises and false papers. On being sent to a screening camp, he revealed his identity, but on being searched, he bit into a cyanide capsule and died shortly after.

Josef Goebbels

Josef Goebbels was one of the most famous and talented propagandists of all time. Through clever manipulation and presentation of the truth, he was able to help Hitler bring the Third Reich to reality.

Goebbels in his office as seen in Signal *magazine.*

Paul Josef Goebbels was born on October 29, 1897, to a poor, but devoutly Catholic working class family who lived in the Rhineland. At the age of seven he fell seriously ill, and following surgery was left with a crippled foot and a left leg that was three inches shorter than the right. This caused him to walk with a pronounced limp, which gave him an real inferiority complex. Although he was rejected out of hand due to his physical condition when he tried to enlist in 1914, he overcame this humiliation and went and went on to study at eight different universities. During this time he received his Ph.D. in German literature from the University of Heidelberg, and had ambitions of becoming an author.

Goebbels joined the Rhineland branch of the Nazi party in 1924, where his literary talents were quickly made use of. He was soon appointed as secretary to Gregor Strasser, the Nazi party organiser in North Germany, and editor for two important party publications, the *Volkische Freiheit* (National Freedom), and the *NS Briefe* (NS Letters). When Hitler saw Goebbels speak publicly, he was very impressed at his ability to work a crowd, and realised that he would be a great asset to the Nazi Party. At first, Goebbels felt that Hitler should not be leading the Nazis, and that they should unite with the Communists. Hitler, however, was not to be put off, and through the use of lies, flattery, charm and deceit soon managed to win Goebbels' loyalty—something he demonstrated until the very end.

In 1926, Hitler named Josef Goebbels party leader of Berlin—a job he performed extremely well. From here he went on to become Nazi Party Propaganda Chief in 1930, where he felt that no method was 'too crude, too low, too brutal.' His work motto became, 'Any lie, frequently repeated, will gradually gain acceptance.' He gave the German people the message that agency called the Reich Chamber of Culture, which controlled all aspects of the press. He ensured that free speech was eliminated, and that the film industry glorified Nazi Stormtroopers and vilified the Jews. Goebbels stayed close to Hitler throughout the war,

Hitler, Magda and Josef Goebbels.

Hitler was on a divine mission, and that they were racially superior to the 'subhuman' Jews and Slavs. Goebbels made the Nazi Party into a pseudo-religious movement and used as many symbolic and ritualistic devices as possible.

Goebbels went on to be appointed Minister of Popular Enlightenment and Propaganda and also created a new and when the end was in sight he took his wife and six children (ages 5 to 13) to the bunker beneath the Reich Chancellery. After Hitler killed himself, Goebbels and his wife arranged that they and their children would be killed by SS orderlies.

MARTIN BORMANN

Martin Bormann was a ruthless manipulator who used every dirty trick in the book to reach the highest levels of the Nazi Party—and through their use even became Hitler's most trusted aide.

He made many enemies as he deviously rose through the ranks of the Nazi hierarchy and became what Hitler called his most 'loyal party comrade'.

Born on June 17, 1900, in Halberstadt, Germany, Martin Bormann was only 14 when World War I began—nevertheless, before it ended he joined up as a artilleryman. After hostilities ceased, he became a member of the Rossback Freikorps, a small extremist right-wing political party. Bormann showed his true colours whilst he was still only in his early twenties, when he took part in the murder of one of his former teachers as the man responsible for the capture and execution of a senior Freikorps member. For this, Bormann served one year in prison, after which he joined the Nazi Party as a press officer. He soon showed promise, and before long had risen to become a business manager.

After marrying the daughter of a senior Nazi Party member, Martin Bormann's career took off, and he became one of the elected Nazi delegates in the Reichstag when Hitler came to power in 1933. He then took a post as Rudolf Hess's personal secretary with the title of Chief of Cabinet in the Office of the Deputy Führer. In this position, he had access to the highest levels of government, and quickly came to Hitler's attention when he realised that extra party funds could be generated by charging royalty fees for the use of Hitler's image on postage stamps. On top of this he managed to create a special fund into which industrialists who were profiting from Nazi rearmament could contribute cash to the Nazi party. Between them, these two ideas raked in million, and unsurprisingly, Hitler was very impressed.

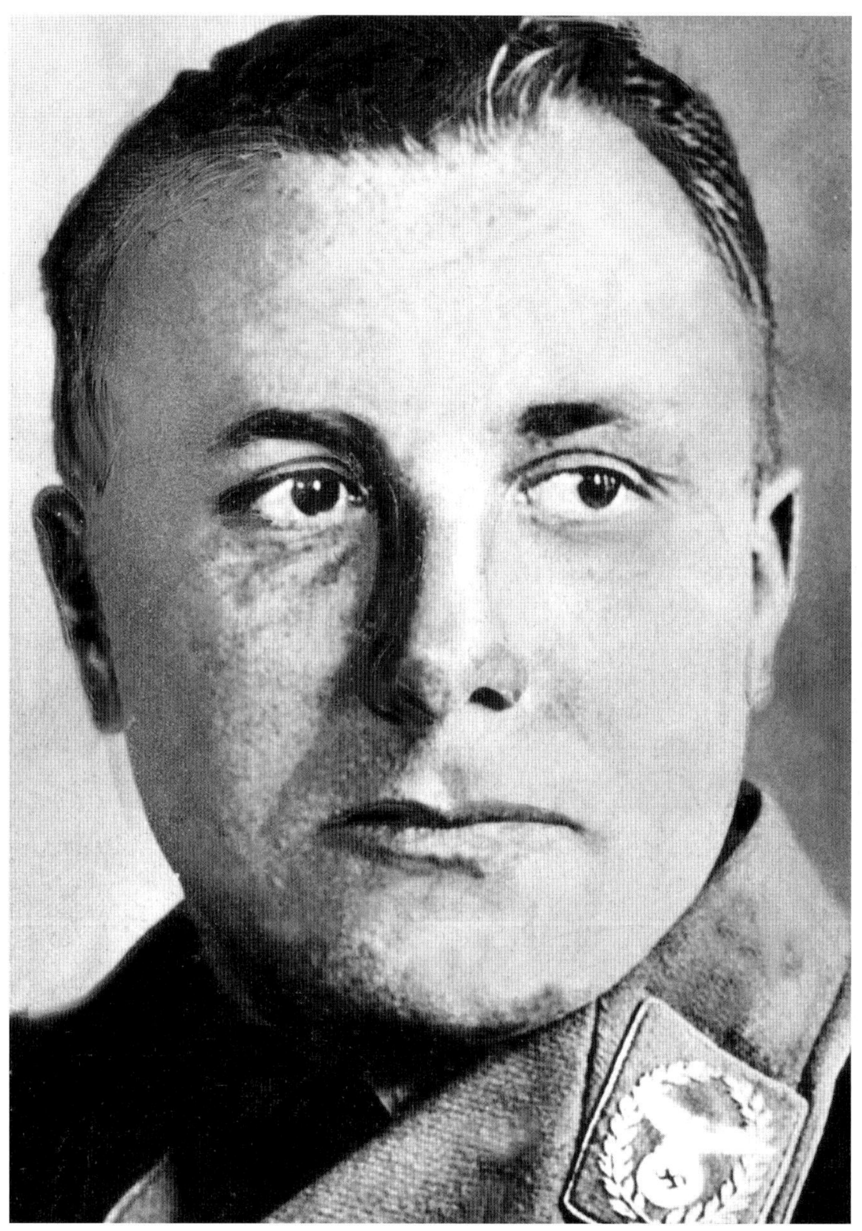

Martin Bormann made himself indispensable to Hitler as his private secretary. His death was not witnessed although in April 1973 a German court formally pronounced him dead after exhuming a skeleton half a mile from Hitler's bunker.

Bormann enjoyed having access to power, and decided that the best way would be to get closer to Hitler. He did this by slowly taking over Hess' duties—he always carried a notebook, and whenever Hitler gave a verbal order or made a suggestion, Bormann wrote his thoughts down and saw to it that they were carried out. In this manner he made himself indispensable, and he became one of Hitler's most trusted aides. Hitler was so angered by Hess's abortive attempt to broker peace with the British that he abolished the post of Deputy Führer which Hess had previously held. In its place he created the role of Head of the Party Chancellery, and gave the position to

Bormann.

In 1943, he was made Secretary to the Führer, and it was in this role that he started to wield real power. Anyone who wanted to see Hitler had to have Bormann's agreement, and to enhance his situation, he created an alliance with Himmler, who had access to the Gestapo's secret files. Having such information to hand, he was a very dangerous man and was not afraid to get involved in power plays with the likes of Göring, Goebbels, and Speer.

Bormann was indiscriminate in his approach to dealing with the Jews, and ensured that they received the worst of treatment in the concentration camps. He also felt that the Catholic church stood in the way of the Nazis, and did his best to suppress the influence of religion in the Third Reich. To do this he saw to it that he was given jurisdiction over all manner of domestic affairs, including the courts and churches.

When the end came in the spring of 1945, Bormann remained with Hitler—even signing his last will and testament and acting as witness to Hitler's marriage to Eva Braun. After Hitler committed suicide, Bormann left the bunker—some say he escaped to South America, others that he was killed by a Russian anti-tank shell while he was trying to escape. This would appear to be backed up by the facts—one of two skeletons dug up in Berlin in 1972 was positively identified as that of Martin Bormann.

Hitler's HQ staff during the attack on the West: to Hitler's left is Jodl and then Bormann.

Reinhard Heydrich

Reinhard Heydrich turned Germany into a terrifying police state and was responsible for the deaths of millions of innocent people.

Reinhard Tristan Eugen Heydrich was born on March 7, 1904, in Halle an der Saale, Germany. His Catholic family was well off, but strongly anti-Semitic. Although his early years were mostly spent studying music, he also joined the Maracker Freikorps and the Deutscher Schutz und Truzbund, both right-wing extremist groups that were highly racist. He was too young to play a part in World War I, but after the war, at the age of eighteen, he became a naval cadet at Germany's main naval base at Kiel. Within four years he rose to the rank of second lieutenant, and became a signals officer on the battleship Schleswig Holstein. He stayed in the navy until April 1931, when Admiral Erich Raeder sentenced him to dismissal for impropriety as a result of seducing the daughter of an influential shipyard director and then spurning her for another woman.

Not long after leaving the navy, Heydrich came to the attention of Himmler, who was looking for someone to set up a counterintelligence branch of the SS. He was given the job, and soon proved to be brilliant in his work, using his cold, calculating mind to invent new methods of trapping, humiliating, and destroying his enemies. His main weapon was a database of dirty secrets that he built up on all manner of people, all stored in a rigorously efficient filing system . These included senior Nazi members as well as their opponents—he obtained information through his own web of informers, which made him especially dangerous. His work was so important to the Nazis that he was promoted to the rank of SS major within the year, and again to SS colonel a year later. His counterintelligence service was renamed as the *Sicherheitsdienst* (Security Service, or SD for short).

The Reichsprotektor of Bohemia and Moravia, Reinhard Heydrich, in Prague in 1941.

Heydrich and Himmler worked together for many years, each depending on the other on their quest for power and control. The partnership proved itself to be especially powerful in June 1934 when the two of them decided that the SA was getting too strong. Although Ernst Rohm was one of Hitler's close personal friends, as head of the SA, he posed a significant threat to both Heydrich and Himmler. The SA was, however, also a threat to Herman Göring. In return for control over the Gestapo, the SD provided false evidence of an intended SA coup—Heydrich then convinced Hitler to countenance a purge of the SA. It was these actions that resulted in the wholesale slaughter that became known as the 'Night of the Long Knives'.

After the threat from the SA was removed, Heydrich built the Gestapo into a massive organisation with even more dirty secrets filed away for future use. Their methods were extreme, and even minor infractions such as anti-Hitler jokes resulted in death sentences. Members of the Gestapo could arrest or murder anyone they wanted, and this instilled a reign of fear that spread throughout Germany. He did favours for Hitler, and as the war progressed continued in his ruthless campaign of terror, all the time acquiring more control over new departments and offices. His reputation was such that he became known as 'the blonde beast' and as 'Himmler's evil genius'.

When the German armies invaded Russia in 1941, Heydrich was responsible for running special killing units—the *Einsatzgruppen*. These units would go to Jewish villages and murder vast numbers of innocent civilians, usually by single shots to the back of the head. By the end of 1941, it was estimated that between the Ukraine, Latvia, Estonia, and Lithuania, almost half a million people had been massacred. When Heydrich was sent into Czechoslovakia to oversee the situation there, he quickly became known as 'The Butcher of Prague' for his barbarous actions. In desperation, the exiled Czech government had two specially trained men parachuted into Czechoslovakia, where with help from the partisans, in December 1941, they managed to assassinate Heydrich with a grenade.

After Heydrich died, Hitler ordered massive reprisals to be made on the local civilian population. He was then succeeded by Ernst Kaltenbrunner, who was a life-long fanatical Nazi. Like Heydrich, he was another brutal man, responsible for the deaths of millions of Jews and political suspects in the concentration camps, as well as the murder of large numbers of prisoners of war. Kaltenbrunner was indicted for war crimes by the International Military Tribunal at Nuremberg and sentenced to death. He was hanged on October 16, 1946.

After Heydrich's assassination there were widespread reprisals but none so terrible than the destruction of Lidice where 172 men and boys over 16 were murdered by Nazi troops. This is a postwar remembrance service for the inhabitants of Lidice.

Hess and Hitler in Munich before World War II.

Rudolf Hess

Rudolf Hess, became Deputy Führer of the Nazi party, and was Adolf Hitler's most devoted follower.

Rudolf Hess was born in Alexandria, Egypt on April 26, 1894, where his father was a successful exporter and wholesaler. He was privately tutored as a child since his father considered the local Protestant school to lack the necessary discipline. Hess was 20 years old when World War I broke out in 1914, and he immediately volunteered for military service. He started out with the 7th Bavarian Field Artillery Regiment, but then transferred to the infantry where he was awarded the Iron Cross, second class for his courage and integrity. After this he managed to get accepted for the Imperial Air Corps, but shortly after having gone through the aeronautical training, the war ended.

When Hess first saw Hitler at a meeting of the German Worker's Party, he was captivated by Hitler's enormous passion. Hess joined the party straight away and from that moment on was dedicated to advancing Hitler's political causes. The two became close friends during the troubled times of the Beer Hall Putsch and the consequent confinement where they shared a cell at Landesberg prison. It was there that Hitler named Hess as his private secretary. When the Nazis gained power in 1933, Hess was given the titles of 'Deputy Führer of the Nazi Party', and 'Reich Minister without Portfolio'.

As the war got underway, Rudolf Hess became a victim of Martin Bormann's political intrigues, and soon found that he had lost most of his power and influence. Knowing that Hitler badly wanted to end hostilities with the British, Hess tried to regain Hitler's approval by embarking on a madcap attempt to negotiate a peace settlement with Churchill by personally flying a Messerschmitt Bf110 fighter plane to Scotland in May 1941. He flew to Scotland because at the Berlin

Hitler revisits Landsberg am Lech, the prison-fortress in which he spent nine months' detention following the Munich Beer-Hall Putsch of 1923. While he was in prison he dictated Mein Kampf (My Struggle) to fellow inmate Rudolf Hess, who would go on to become his private secretary.

After his flight to Britain, Hess was kept in prison—at first in Britain and postwar in Spandau—until he killed himself in 1987.

Olympics of 1936 he had met Douglas Douglas-Hamilton who became the Duke of Hamilton. Hess had already tried to negotiate a peace with Britain through the duke in 1940, and still hoped that his personal contact would do the trick. The duke had not replied to Hess's earlier advances on the advice of British Intelligence, and when Hess arrived in Britain after bailing out of his aircraft, he was immediately imprisoned, his mission having failed completely.

Churchill—who always viewed Hess as a medical and not a criminal case—ensured he was treated with dignity and he was imprisoned in the Tower of London.

In Germany, Hitler felt betrayed by someone he had previously considered to be a close personal friend—second in line to succeed Hitler after Göring. Branded a madman by his erstwhile colleagues, Hess remained as a prisoner of the Allies for the duration of the war. At the Nuremberg Trials he was sentenced to life imprisonment in Spandau Allied Military Prison, where he hanged himself on August 17, 1987.

The alte Kämpfer (old fighters—the old guard) were those early members of the NSDAP who had fought alongside Hitler in the 1920s. Many of them received positions of importance after 1933. The November 9, 1923, march from the Munich Beer-Hall toward the centre of the city, the Marienplatz, was reenacted in later years—as here in these 1934 photographs of the anniversary.

Sixteen of Hitler's companions died on November 9, 1923, when police ended the Beer-Hall Putsch. This parade on the Royal Square in Munich passes the Ehrentempel—*the temple of honour. The inscription below was placed on a monument to the fallen in the* Feldherrn Halle *(the hall of heroes) in Munich. It commemorates the names of the 16 fallen.*

Flags were of great importance to the Nazis and each year at the Nuremberg Rallies Hitler consecrated new colours—as here in 1934. He did this by grasping the Blutfahne *(blood banner), so-called because it had been carried on November 9, and covered in the blood of the 16 martyrs, and touching the new colours.*

Portrait of Alfred Rosenberg, the Nazis' ideologist and Reichminister for the Eastern Occupied territories where he arranged the extermination of Jews and slave labour gangs. He was executed following the Nuremberg Trials.

Alfred Rosenberg

Alfred Rosenberg was a propagandist who was responsible for many of the Nazis policies towards the Jews. He also formed special units which ransacked Jewish properties—especially museums and libraries for art treasures and other valuable artefacts.

Alfred Rosenberg was born in Estonia (which at the time was part of Russia) on January 12, 1893, into the family of a cobbler. As a student he studied architecture in Moscow until the revolution in 1917, whereupon he returned home and got involved in counter revolutionary politics. This resulted in him having to flee to Germany to avoid arrest, where he joined the National Socialist Party in 1919. As a skilled propagandist he started writing all manner of official party material, and in 1921 was also made editor of the official Nazi party newspaper, the *Völkischer Beobachter*.

Rosenberg argued strongly that preserving German racial purity was of paramount importance, and that the threat from the Bolsheviks justified Germany invading Poland and Russia. He then went on to found the Militant League for German Culture in 1929, and in 1930 was elected to the Reichstag. The same year he published a manuscript called 'The Myth of the Twentieth Century', in which he claimed that there were two opposing races—the Aryans and the Jews. The Aryans, he said, were responsible for the creation of everything of cultural value, whereas the Jewish race sought to pervert or destroy the very same things. He became head of the Nazi party foreign policy office in 1933, where he called for the Treaty of Versailles to be rescinded.

Over the next few years he continued to push his extremist racial beliefs, and his advocacy of German expansion. Hitler was so impressed with his abilities in this area that he appointed Rosenberg to be head of the Hohe Schule, the 'University of Nazism' in 1940. Under the guise of establishing this spurious academic institution, Rosenberg sent units out to seize books from Jewish libraries as well as art treasures from Jewish homes and public buildings. After the invasion of the Soviet Union had begun in 1941, he became Reich Minister for the Occupied Eastern Territories.

Although Rosenberg operated at the very highest levels of power, and was a supporter of the repression of the Jews, he did try to minimise the harsh treatment of other races in the occupied Eastern Territories. This brought him into direct conflict with the SS, and as a result the overall amount of influence he wielded was reduced. This did not help him when he was captured by the Allies at the end of the war and tried at Nuremberg. He was found guilty on many counts, including war-crimes and crimes against humanity. He was sentenced to death and executed on the morning of October 16, 1946.

Albert Speer

Albert Speer was an architect who rose to become one of Adolf Hitler's closest colleagues. He was tasked with keeping the German war effort running in spite of allied air bombardment and naval blockades. His organisational skills kept the war going for at least a year longer than it otherwise would have, at an untold cost in human lives and misery.

Albert Speer, was born in Mannheim on 19th March, 1905. His father was an architect, and after following the usual schooling that the child of a professional family would receive, he went on to study architecture at the Munich Institute of Technology and at the Berlin-Charlottenburg Institute. He became an architect in 1927, and in 1932 became a member of the Nazi Party (NSDAP) after hearing Hitler speak. Shortly afterwards he also became a member of the SS—as a consequence of this he met Adolf Hitler in July 1933, whereupon he was given the task of organising the 1934 Nuremberg Rally. This included the design of the parade grounds, searchlights, and banners, factors all used to great effect in the *Triumph of the Will*, the famous film created by Leni Riefenstahl. Speer excelled at such matters, and Hitler was so impressed with his skills he was appointed as the Führer's personal architect. Speer was given many important commissions including the German exhibit at the Paris Exhibition in 1937, the Reich Chancellery in Berlin and the Party Palace in Nuremberg.

Speer's efficiency was such that Hitler came to rely on him for many important matters, and in 1942 he took over from the engineer Fritz Todt

Hitler visits the site of the House of German Art in Munich. Albert Speer is on the right of the photograph.

An older Albert Speer seen with Admiral Karl Dönitz and Generaloberst Gustav Jodl.

as minister for armaments. In doing so was given charge of the Organisation Todt, which used forced labour for the construction of strategic roads and defences. When Göring fell from favour in 1943, Speer also took over as planner of the German war economy. Under his management, German economic production went up, even in the face of the massive amount of Allied bombing. Speer gained a reputation as a 'Good Nazi'—in part, this was due to the fact that he did his best to stop Hitler from destroying German lands and properties in a scorched earth policy ahead of the advancing allied and Soviet armies. Had these plans gone ahead, it would have left Germany ruined.

After the war was over, Speer was sentenced to 20 years in prison at the Nuremberg trials. On his release he wrote his memoirs, wherein he stated that he should have known more about what was going on, but didn't; he died a wealthy man in 1981.

Baldur von Shirach

Baldur von Schirach was born in Berlin on March 9, 1907, to an aristocratic German father and an American mother. After a privileged upbringing, he joined the Nazi Party in 1924 whilst at the University of Munich where he was studying Germanic folklore and art history. His strong socialist ideals meant that he did not fit in with his aristocratic peers, and he became a strong opponent of the rich. The same political beliefs also made him a militant opponent of Christianity throughout his career.

One of von Schirach's great attributes was his ability to inspire enthusiasm in the young, and this combined with his devotion to Hitler, made him a natural choice as the leader of the National Socialist German Students' League, a post he took in 1929. Two years later, he was also appointed as Reich Youth Leader of the NSDAP. Von Schirach was also an excellent organiser, and the endless propaganda helped by the vast youth rallies he staged drew hundreds of thousands of eager new members to the party fold. Out of this massive influx of young blood he built the Hitler Youth or Hitlerjugend into a massive cult—in 1936 it had six million members. The core principles he encouraged were designed to create a new cadre of soldiers ready for Hitler's war machine. These ideals included character, discipline, obedience and leadership, all held together with a powerful mixture of pagan romanticism, militarism and naive patriotism. They were told they were the basis for a new Aryan race of supermen or Übermensch.

Nuremberg: inspection of the Hitlerjugend. Behind Hitler is its head, Baldur von Schirach.

Although Baldur von Schirach was incredibly successful in these efforts, it did not make him immune to the conspiracies of other high level Nazis. Jealous of his popularity, he became a target for the likes of Martin Bormann. This undermined his credibility, and he was relieved of his command of the Hitler Youth. He was made Governor of Vienna, Austria in August 1940, and Bormann continued to feed Hitler with misinformation about von Schirach's activities, especially his pleas for better treatment for the people of eastern European. Von Schirach also voiced his disapproval of the manner in which the Jews were being deported, but the fact that he was involved in the removal of 185,000 Jews from Vienna to Poland stood against him after the war. At the Nuremberg trials he denied all knowledge of genocide, denounced

Russian guards on duty outside Spandau prison. Seven Nazi war criminals served sentences in Spandau, each given a number. 1 was Baldur von Schirach; 2 Karl Dönitz; 3 von Neurath; 4 Erich Raeder; 5 Albert Speer; 6 Walther Funk; 7 Rudolf Hess.

Hitler as 'a million-fold murderer' and called Auschwitz 'the most devilish mass murder in history'. He was sentenced to 20 years in prison for crimes against humanity, and was released in 1966 after serving them. He wrote in his memoirs that he should have done more to prevent the establishment of the concentration camps. He also accepted responsibility for helping to poison a whole generation of youth, and considered it his duty to stop any ideas of resurrecting Nazism. He died in August 1974.

Karl Döenitz

Karl Dönitz is unusual in that he not only attained an extremely high rank—Grossadmiral (Admiral of the Fleet in Royal Navy terms)—in the Kriegsmarine but that he became Hitler's nominated successor .Born in Grünau bei Berlin on September 16, 1891, after school he joined the navy and served during World War I initially with the surface fleet. He was on the Breslau when it and the Goeben broke through the British Mediterranean fleet to reach Turkish waters in 1914. He continued to serve in warships until October 1916, when he joined the submarine fleet. And it was as Commander in Chief of Submarines during World War II that he would make his mark.

When the war started in 1939, Dönitz was chosen to head the U-boat arm—at that time consisting of only 50 boats, many of them shorter-range types. However, the force immediately proved successful and Dönitz would go on to develop the tactics that brought Britain to her knees. Indeed, had it not been for the fact that Britain was able to read much of the German Enigma coded transmissions Dönitz's U-boat arm could well have won the war in the west for Hitler.

In his will, Adolf Hitler chose Dönitz as his successor as German Head of State, a choice that shows how distrustful Hitler had become of Göring and Himmler in the final days of the war in Europe. Significantly, Dönitz was not to become Führer, but rather President of Germany (Reichspräsident), a post Hitler had abolished. Propaganda Minister Joseph Goebbels was to become Head of Government and Chancellor of Germany (Reichskanzler). After Hitler committed suicide on April 30, 1945, Dönitz ruled only for a few weeks, holding office through the final surrender on May 8 until his arrest by the British on May 23 at Flensburg. He devoted most of his efforts to trying to ensure that German troops surrendered to the Americans and not to the Soviets. Following the war, Dönitz went on trial as a war criminal in the Nuremberg Trials. Unlike many of the other defendants, he was not charged with crimes against humanity. However, he was charged with being involved with waging of aggressive war, conspiracy to wage aggressive war and crimes against the laws of war. Specifically, he faced charges of waging unrestricted submarine warfare and of issuing an order after the Laconia incident not to rescue survivors from ships attacked by submarine. He served ten years as prisoner number two in Spandau prison, being released on October 1, 1956. He died on December 24, 1980.

HANS FRANK

Born in Karlsruhe on May 23, 1900, Frank was a Nazi lawyer—Hitler's lawyer—who became the governor of the Generalgouvernement of Poland from 1939 to the end of the war.

He served for only the last year of World War I and joined the Freikorps afterwards, Frank joined the Deutsche Arbeiterpartei in 1919, and became a member of the NSDAP when it was absorbed. He took part in the Munich Beer-Hall Putsch as a stormtrooper. He passed the bar exams in 1926 and from then on defended brownshirts in court—a full-time job as there were over 40,000 such trials between 1925 and 1933. Throughout the 1920s, Frank served as Adolf Hitler's personal lawyer and the head of the legal department of the NSDAP.

Frank lost his importance as a lawyer after the Nazis reached power in 1933. He was given a number of positions including Bavarian Minister of Justice and Reichsleiter of the NSDAP.

After the defeat of Poland in September 1939, the Germans and Russians split the country into three: the western went to the greater reich; the eastern went to the Soviet Union, leaving the central area—the Generalgouvernement, a semi-independent administrative unit. Frank was appointed governor-general of the Generalgouvernement. However, Frank did not hold great power there. He was the most important administrator in the region; but while he managed to get Hermann Göring to cooperate with him regarding the region's economy, the SS took charge of the extermination of Jews in the Generalgouvernement. Hitler meant for the Generalgouvernement to be used as a "racial dumping ground," an endless supply of slave labor, and a site for the mass extermination of European Jewry. Frank did not oppose these goals, but he hated others infringing on his domain. Thus, he went back and forth, sometimes opposing and sometimes supporting the inflow of Jews and Poles who had been expelled from German-occupied areas and the mass murder of Jews. He very much wanted to please Hitler, but he also wanted to build up his own power base. This conflict led to his downfall.

In March 1942 Frank was stripped of all power over racial and police issues. He then began to openly criticize SS policies, leading Hitler to remove Frank of his party positions. Hitler, though, would not allow Frank to resign, so Frank stayed in the position of governor-general until he was forced to flee from the advancing Soviet army. After the war, Frank was tried and hanged at Nuremberg. His official diary still serves as an important source for World War II historians.

Wilhelm Frick

Wilhelm Frick was born in Germany in 1877. A police officer in Munich, he joined the National Socialist German Workers Party (NSDAP) and took part in the Beer Hall Putsch. Along with Adolf Hitler was found guilty and was imprisoned for his role in the attempted putsch.

In 1924 Frick was elected to the Reichstag where he associated with the NSDAP radicals led by Gregor Strasser. He became the first Nazi to hold high office when he was appointed as Minister of the Interior in the state of Thuringia.

When Adolf Hitler became Chancellor in 1933 he appointed Frick as his Minister of the Interior and was responsible for operating the Enabling Act. He also drafted the Nuremberg Laws, that began the persecution of the Jews in Germany.

Frick was involved in a struggle with Heinrich Himmler and the Schutzstaffel (SS) and in 1943 lost his job as Minister of the Interior. Adolf Hitler now appointed him the Protector of Bohemia and Moravia, a post he held until the end of the Second World War.

Frick was accused of crimes against humanity at the Nuremberg War Crimes Trial. At his trial Frick argued that he had never intended the Nuremberg Laws to be used for mass murder, although he accepted that this is what happened. Wilhelm Frick was found guilty and executed on 1st October, 1946.

WALTHER FUNK

Walther Funk, the son of a businessman, was born in Trakehnen, Germany, on 18th August, 1890. After studying economics at university he became a financial journalist.

Funk joined the National Socialist German Workers Party (NSDAP) in 1931. He became an adviser to Adolf Hitler and encouraged him to move away from the radical anti-capitalist views of Gregor Strasser and Ernst Röhm.

After the Night of the Long Knives Funk's influence grew and in 1937 he was appointed by Hitler as Minister of Economics. Two years later he succeeded Hjalmar Schacht as President of the Reichsbank.

During the Second World War Funk collaborated with Heinrich Himmler in depositing money looted from the Jewish community.

At the end of the war Funk was captured by Allied troops. Found guilty of crimes against humanity at the Nuremberg War Crimes Trial he was sentenced to life imprisonment. In May 1957, Funk was released from prison because of ill-health and died in Düsseldorf on 31st May, 1960.

Alfred Jodl

Alfred Jodl was born in Würzburg, Germany, on 10th May, 1890. He attended cadet school and 1910 joined a field military regiment in the German Army.

Soon after the outbreak of the First World War Jodl suffered a severe thigh wound. He recovered and saw further action on the Western Front and the Eastern Front. Disillusioned by Germany's defeat he considered leaving the army and becoming a doctor.

In 1935 Jodl was promoted to the rank of general major. After the Anschluss he was sent to Vienna as head of the 44th Artillery Command. He returned to Germany and in September he took part in the invasion of Poland.

A strong supporter of the National Socialist German Workers Party (NSDAP), Jodl worked closely with Adolf Hitler and in October, 1939, was appointed chief of operations. In January, 1944, Jodl was promoted to the rank of Generaloberst.

Jodl came close to be killed when the bomb exploded in the July Plot. He recovered and in May, 1945, signed the unconditional surrender of Germany to the Allies. Soon afterwards he was arrested and charged with war crimes.

At the Nuremberg War Crimes Trial Jodl was charged of approving orders that violated the rules of war. Alfred Jodl was found guilty and hanged on 16th October, 1946.

Ernst Kaltenbrunner

Ernst Kaltenbrunner, the son of a lawyer, was born in Austria on 4th October, 1903. He got a doctorate in law from Graz University in 1925 and set up as a lawyer in Linz.

Kaltenbrunner joined the Austrian Nazi Party in 1932 and worked closely with Arthur Seyss-Inquart and Adolf Eichmann. Kaltenbrunner became head of the Austrian SS in 1934 but soon afterwards was arrested and accused of being involved in the assassination of Engelbert Dollfuss. Found guilty of conspiracy and was sentenced to six months in prison.

After Anschluss Kaltenbrunner was elected to the Reichstag and became minister for state security as well as police chief in Vienna. During the next three years Kaltenbrunner served as Commander-in-Chief of the Schutzstaffel (SS) in Vienna.

In April 1941 Kaltenbrunner was appointed Lieutenant-General of Police. He impressed Heinrich Himmler and when Reinhard Heydrich was assassinated in May, 1942, Kaltenbrunner was appointed as head of the SD (Sicherheitsdienst). In this position he not only controlled the Gestapo but also the concentration camp system and was responsible for carrying out the Final Solution.

Nearly seven feet tall, with deep scars on his face from his student duelling days, Kaltenbrunner appeared to obtain pleasure from his work and took personal interest in the different methods of killing the inmates in the extermination camps.

As well as the hunting down and extermination of several million Jews Kaltenbrunner was also responsible for the murder of Allied parachutists and prisoners-of-war.

With the Red Army closing in on Germany, Kaltenbrunner gave orders for all prisoners in extermination camps to be killed and then fled south but was captured by Allied troops. Accused of crimes against humanity at the Nuremberg War Crimes Trial he was found guilty and executed on 1st October, 1946.

WILHELM KEITEL

Wilhelm Keitel, the son of a landowner, was born in Hanover on 22nd September 1882. He joined the German Army and in 1902 became a second lieutenant in the 46th Field Artillery.

Keitel had reached the rank of captain by the outbreak of the First World War. In September 1914 Keitel was seriously wounded by a shell splinter. After returning to duty he became a battery commander before being appointed to the General Staff in March 1915. He also served as an officer with XIX Reserve Corps (1916-17) and the 199th Infantry Division (1917) before returning to the General Staff in Berlin in December 1917.

After the war Keitel was a member of the right-wing terrorist Freikorps group and served on the frontier with Poland in 1919. He remained in the army and spent three years as an instructor at the School of Cavalry at Hanover (1920-23). This was followed by a spell with the 6th Artillery Regiment.

Assigned to the Troop Office he was promoted to lieutenant colonel in February 1929. Later that year he became head of the Organizations Department. In this role he was involved in secret preparations to triple the size of the German Army.

In January 1933, Adolf Hitler gained power and immediately Keitel's old friend, Werner von Blomberg, was appointed Minister of Defence. Soon afterwards Blomberg introduced him to Hitler. Keitel was impressed and became a devoted supporter of the new leader.

In February 1938 Keitel became Commander-in-Chief of the High Command of the Armed Forces (OKW). He now arranged to have his friend, Heinrich von Brauchitsch, appointed as Commander-in-Chief of the Army.

During the Second World War Keitel, Alfred Jodl and Walther Warlimont were the most important figures in the OKW. He was a loyal supporter of Hitler's policies and after the invasion of Poland he issued orders to the Schutz Staffeinel (SS) and the Gestapo to exterminate the country's Jews.

Keitel advised against the Western Offensive and Operation Barbarossa but quickly backed down when Hitler responded aggressively. Both times he tried to resign but Hitler refused him permission to go.

In May 1941 Keitel signed the Commissar Order which instructed German field commanders to execute Communist Party officials immediately they were captured. In July 1941 he signed another order giving Heinrich Himmler the power to implement his racial program in the Soviet Union.

In September 1942 Keitel and Alfred Jodl defended Field Marshal Wilhelm List against the criticisms of Adolf Hitler. This resulted in Jodl being sacked and for many months afterwards Hitler refused to shake hands with Keitel. This was the last time that Keitel was to challenge Hitler's military decisions. He was now referred to by other officers as "Lakaitel" (the nodding ass).

Over the next two years Keitel issued orders for the execution of striking workers, the extermination of Jews and the killing of captured partisans. He also suggested that German civilians should be encouraged to lynch captured Allied airman.

After the war Keitel was arrested and tried at Nuremberg as a major war criminal. In court his main defence was that he was merely obeying orders claiming that he was "never permitted to make decisions". Found guilty he was executed on 16th October, 1946. His autobiography, In Service of the Reich, was published after his death.

Konstantin von Neurath

Konstantin von Neurath was born in Klen-Glattbach, Germany, on 2nd February, 1873. After studying law at the University of Berlin he entered the German foreign service in 1903. He von Papen appointed him Foreign Minister. He retained the post under Kurt von Schleicher and Adolf Hitler.

Neurath held right-wing opinions conservative views but had doubts about Hitler's aggressive foreign policy. part in the rebellion to be executed.

Hitler felt that Neurath did not deal harshly enough with the resistance movement in Czechoslovakia and in September, 1941, replaced him with Reinhard Heydrich.

Premier Benito Mussolini of Italy and Chancellor Adolf Hitler of Germany, pictured as they met in Venice recently, where it is believed the two dictators discussed armaments and other vital questions affecting the political situation of Europe. Baron Von Neurath is seen at the right.

was a member of the consular staff in London from 1903 to 1908, before returning to Berlin.

He joined the German Army in the First World War and as a captain won the Iron Cross. After being badly wounded he returned to diplomatic service in Turkey.

After the war Neurath served as Minister to Denmark and Ambassador to Italy. Following a period as Ambassador to Britain (1930-32) Franz Hitler kept him in position as he gave the government respectability. In March 1938 Hitler replaced Neurath with Joachim von Ribbentrop when he complained that the current policy would result in war.

In 1939 Adolf Hitler appointed Neurath as Protector of Czechoslovakia. When Czech students protested against Nazi rule Neurath closed all the universities in the country. He also ordered nine of the students who took

Neurath was captured by Allied troops at the end of the Second World War. At the Nuremberg War Trial he was found guilty of war crimes and sentenced to fifteen years in prison. After serving eight years he was released on account of his poor health. Konstantin von Neurath died on 14th August, 1956.

Erich Raeder

Erich Raeder, the son of a headmaster, was born in Wandsbek, Schleswig-Holstein, on 24th April, 1876. After a good classical education he entered the Imperial Navy in 1894. He made rapid progress and became Chief of Staff to Franz von Hipper in 1912. During the First World War he saw action and in 1928 was promoted to admiral and head of the German Navy.

Raeder disliked the domestic policies of the National Socialist German Workers Party (NSDAP) but supported Adolf Hitler in his attempts to restore Germany as a great power. In 1939 Hitler promoted Raeder to the rank of grand admiral, the first German to hold this post since Alfred von Tirpitz.

Raeder strategy was to build a German Navy that could challenge the British Navy. This brought him into conflict with Hermann Göring who as director of the German economy directed more resources to the Luftwaffe than the navy.

In October 1939 Raeder sent Adolf Hitler a proposal for capturing Denmark and Norway. He argued that Germany would not be able to defeat Britain unless it created naval bases in these countries. In April 1940 Hitler gave permission for this move but he was disappointed by the heavy losses that the German Navy suffered during the achievement of this objective.

Raeder supported Operation Sealion, the planned German invasion of Britain, but argued that first the Luftwaffe had to gain air superiority. When Hermann Göring failed to win the Battle of Britain Reader advised Hitler to call off the invasion. He was also a strong opponent of Operation Barbarossa.

Adolf Hitler grew increasingly disillusioned with the performance of the German Navy and after the Lützow and Admiral Hipper failed to stop a large Arctic convoy he accused his commander of incompetence. Raeder resigned in January, 1943 and was replaced by Karl Dönitz as Commander in Chief of the navy.

At the Nuremberg War Crimes Trial Raeder was found guilty of conspiring to wage aggressive war and was sentenced to life imprisonment. He was released in 1955 and in retirement wrote his memoirs Mein Leben (1957). Erich Raeder died in Kiel, on 6th November, 1960.

Joachim von Ribbentrop

Joachim von Ribbentrop (April 30, 1893 - October 16, 1946) was the German Foreign Minister from 1938 until 1945.

Ribbentrop was born in Wesel, Niederrhein, as the son of an officer. Fluent in French and English, Ribbentrop lived several years abroad. He served in the Army during World War I, finally as a first lieutenant, and was awarded the Iron Cross. He then became a diplomat, stationed in Constantinople. A wealthy wine merchant, he joined the National Socialist party in 1932. Two years earlier, in 1930, he had met and impressed Adolf Hitler with his knowledge of foreign affairs. He became Hitler's favourite foreign policy advisor and was a great admirer of Hitler. In 1933 he was given the title of SS-Standartenführer.

He was Minister Plenipotentiary at Large (1935 - 1936) and negotiated the Anglo-German Naval Agreement in 1935 and the Anti-Comintern Pact in 1936, in August 1936 he was appointed Ambassador to Britain. While in Britain, his son, Rudolf von Ribbentrop, attended the Westminster School in London. In 1938 he succeeded Konstantin von Neurath as Foreign Minister in the German government. He played a role in the German annexation of Bohemia and Moravia (1938), in the conclusion of the Russo-German nonaggression pact, the Molotov-Ribbentrop Pact in 1939, and in the diplomatic action surrounding the attack on Poland.

At the end of World War II, Ribbentrop was dismissed by Admiral Karl Dönitz, but he was a defendant at the Nuremberg Trials and was found guilty by the enemy of all charges they put against him. Since Hermann Göring had committed suicide a few hours prior to the time of execution, Ribbentrop was the first prisoner of war to be hanged on the night of October 16, 1946. His last words were (spoken in German): "God protect Germany! My last wish is that Germany realize its entity and that an understanding be reached between the East and the West. I wish peace to the world."

In 1953 Ribbentrop's memoirs Zwischen London und Moskau were published.

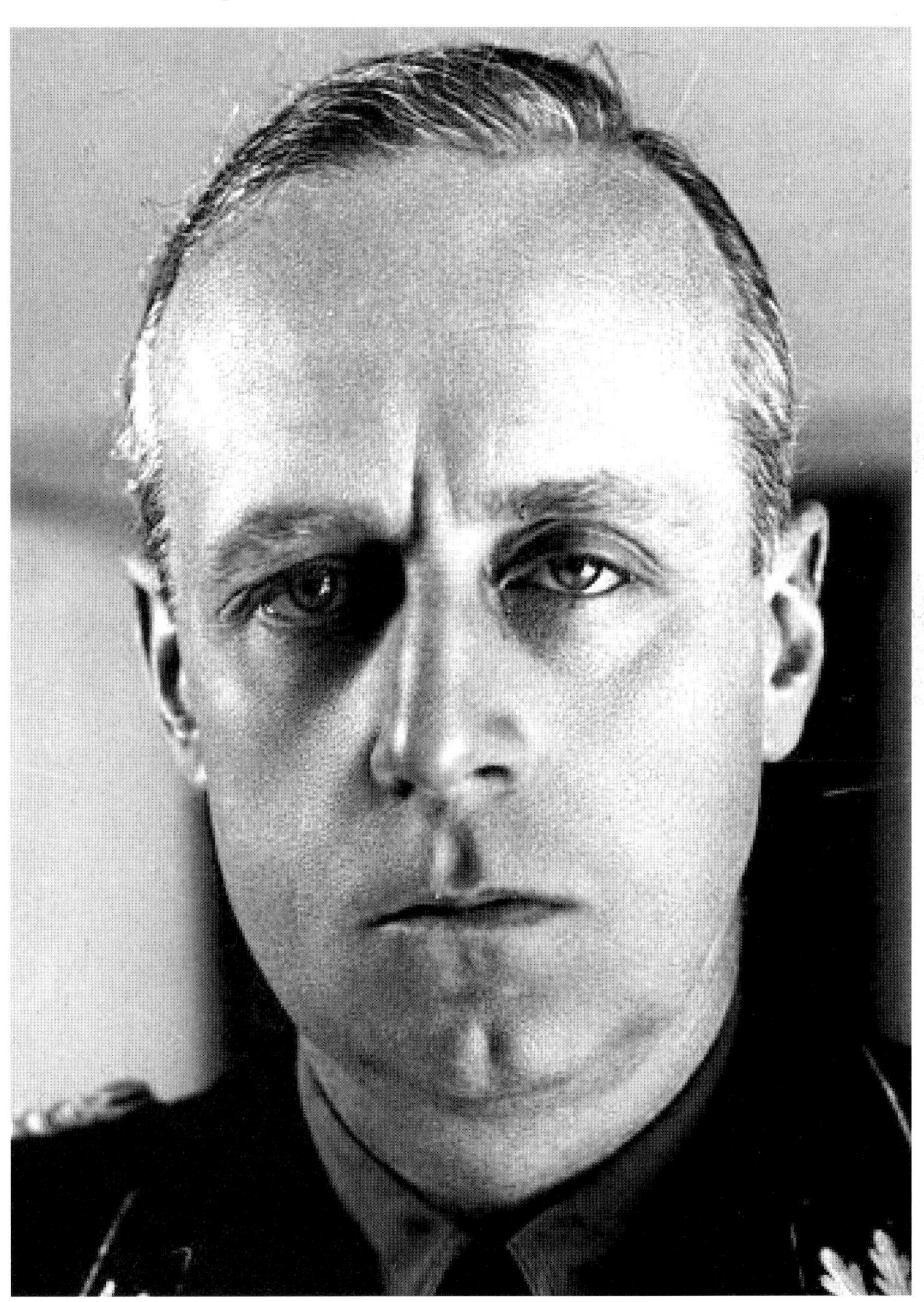

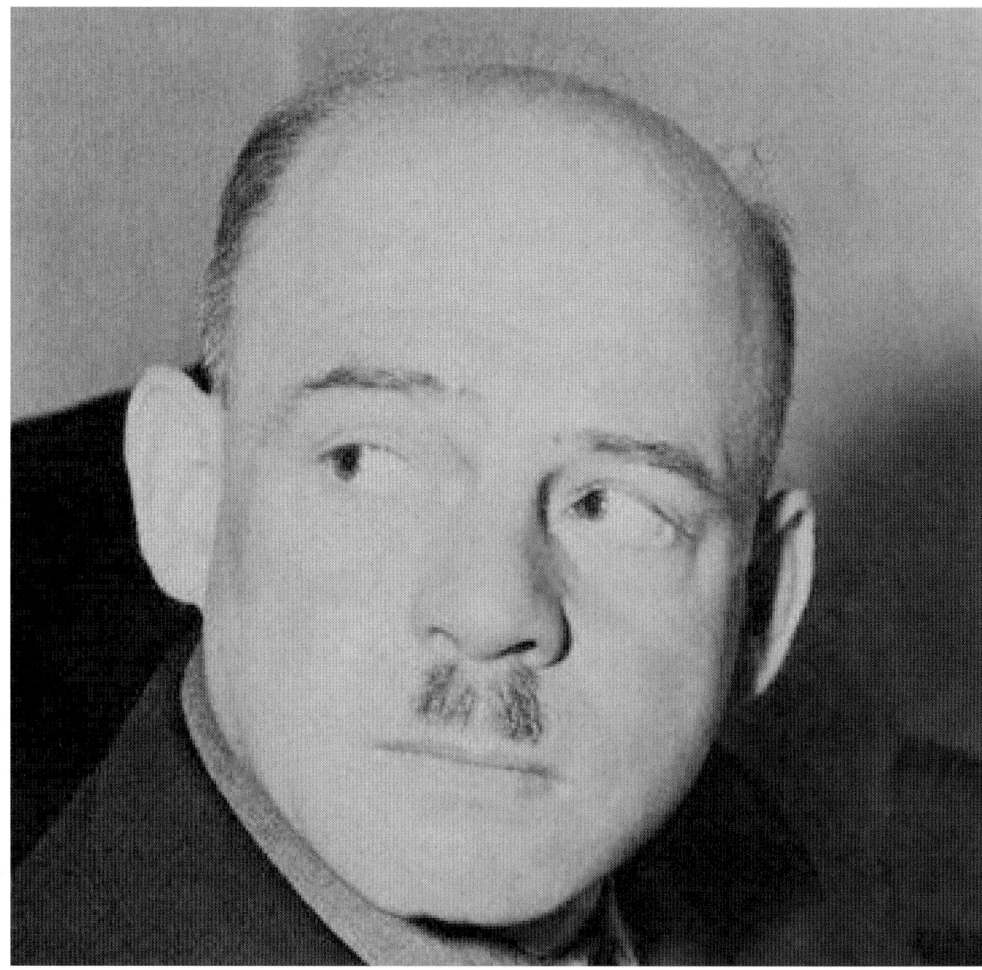

Fritz Sauckel

Fritz Sauckel (Ernst Friedrich Christoph Sauckel, October 27, 1894 - October 16, 1946) was a senior government official in Nazi Germany. He was General Plenipotentiary for the Employment of Labour from 1942 until the end of the war.

Born in Haßfurt-am-Main, near Bamberg, the only child of a postman and a seamstress. He was educated at local schools and left early when his mother fell ill. He joined the merchant marine of Norway and Sweden, aged just fifteen. He went on to sail throughout the world and rose to the rank of Vollmatrose. At the outbreak of WW I he was on a German vessel en route to Australia when the vessel was captured and he was interned in France from August 1914 until November 1919.

He returned to Germany and found factory work in Schweinfurt. He studied engineering in Ilmenau from 1922 to 1923. He joined the NSDAP in 1923 (member 1,395). He also married in that year and went on to have ten children. He remained a party member over its dissolution and publicly rejoined in 1925. Sauckel was appointed party Gauleiter of Thüringia in 1927 and became a member of the regional government in 1929. Following the Nazi seizure of power in 1933 he was promoted to Reich Regent of Thuringia and Reichstag member. He was also given a honorary rank of Obergruppenführer in the SA and the SS in 1934.

During WW II he was Reich defense commissioner for the Kassel district (Re ichsverteidigungskommissar Wehrkreis IX) before being appointed General Plenipotentiary for the Employment of Labour (Generbevollmächtigter für den Arbeitseinsatz) on March 21, 1942, on the recommendation of Albert Speer. He worked directly under Hitler through the Four-Year Plan Office. He directed and controlled German labour. In response to increased demands he met the requirement for manpower with people from the occupied territories. Voluntary numbers were insufficient and forced recruitment was introduced within a few months. Of the 5 million workers brought to Germany, around 200,000 came voluntarily. The majority of the acquired workers originated from the Eastern territories, where the methods used to gain workers were reportedly very harsh.

He was a defendant at the Nuremberg Trials accused of conspiracy to commit crimes against peace; planning, initiating and waging wars of aggression; war crimes and crimes against humanity. He defended the Arbeitseinsatz as "nothing to do with exploitation. It is an economic process for supplying labour". He denied that it was slave labour or that it was common to deliberately work people to death (extermination by labour) or to mistreat them.

He was found guilty of war crimes and crimes against humanity, and together with a number of colleagues, he was hanged on October 16, 1946. His last words were recorded as "Ich sterbe unschuldig, mein Urteil ist ungerecht. Gott beschütze Deutschland!"

Julius Striecher

Julius Streicher (February 12, 1885 - October 16, 1946) was a prominent Nazi prior to and during World War II. He was the publisher of the Nazi Der Stürmer newspaper, which was to become a part of the Nazi propaganda machine. The newspaper was controversial even in Nazi circles because of its pornographic obsessions and sensationalism. His publishing firm released an anti-Semitic children's book Der Giftpilz (trans. "The Poisonous Mushroom").

During the time of the Munich Beer Hall Putsch of 1923, Streicher became friendly with Adolf Hitler and became an active advocate for him.

He was executed following due process at the Nuremberg war trials in 1946. He shouted 'Heil Hitler!' just before the trap door opened beneath him.

Reich Party Leaders Meet. Nuremberg, Germany: Reichminister Hermann Goering (right) and Julius Streicher, Nazi Jew-baiter No. 1, exchange greetings when meeting at Nuremberg for the 10th Nazi Party Congress.

Arthur Seyss Inquart

Arthur Seyss-Inquart (July 22, 1892 - October 16, 1946) was a prominent Nazi official in Austria and for wartime Germany in Poland and the Netherlands.

He was born in Stonarov, Moravia, then part of Austria-Hungary. He moved with his parents to Vienna in 1907 and later went to study law at the University of Vienna. At the start of World War I, he enlisted with the Austrian Army in August 1914 and was given a commission with the Tyrolean Kaiserjäger and served in Russia, Romania and also Italy. He was decorated for bravery on a number of occasions and while recovering from wounds in 1917 he completed his final examinations for his degree.

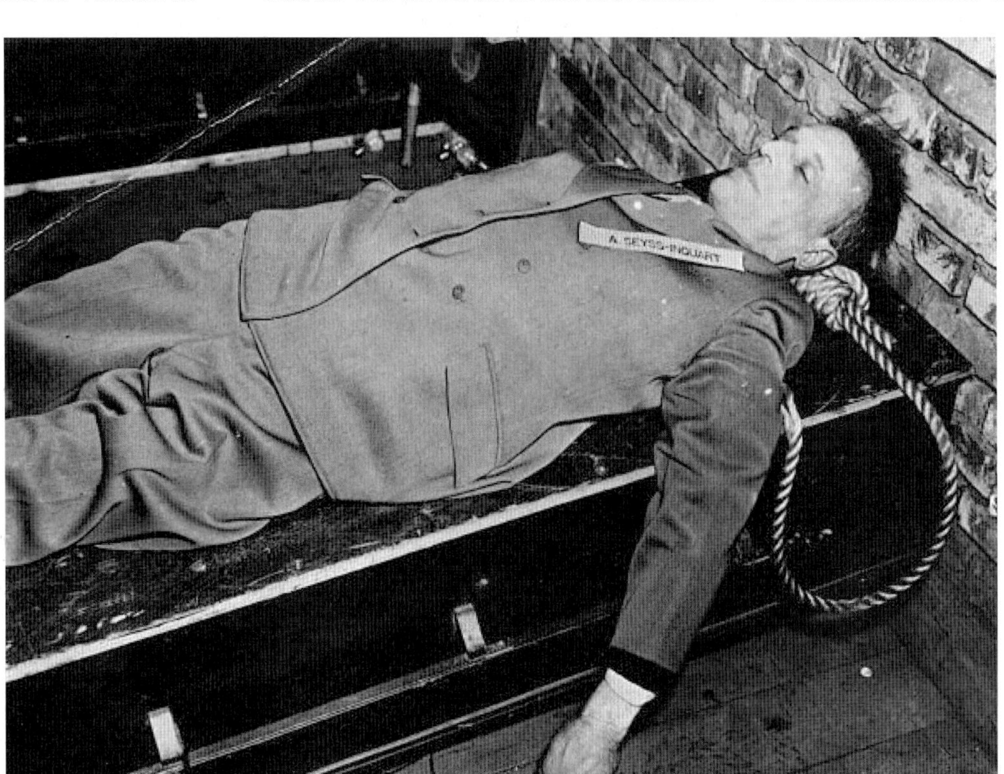

He liaised between the Austrians and Germany for the Anschluss and he joined the German Nazi party in May 1938. He drafted the law reducing Austria to a province of Germany and remained head (Reichsstatthalter) of the newly named Ostmark, with Ernst Kaltenbrunner his chief minister and Burckel as Commissioner for the Reunion of Austria (concerned with the "Jewish Question"). Seyss-Inquart also received an honorary SS rank of "Gruppenführer" and in May 1939 he was made a Minister without portfolio.

Following the invasion of Poland, Seyss-Inquart became administrative chief for Southern Poland, but did not take up that post before the General Government was created, in which he became a deputy to the Governor General Hans Frank. It is claimed that he was involved in the movement of Polish Jews into ghettoes, in the seizure of strategic supplies and in the "extraordinary pacification" of the resistance movement.

Following the capitulation of the Low Countries he was appointed Reichskommissar for the Occupied Netherlands in May 1940, charged with directing the civil administration, with creating close economic collaboration with Germany and with defending the interests of the Reich. He supported the Dutch NSB and allowed them to create a paramilitary Landwacht, which acted as an auxiliary police force. Other political parties were banned in late 1941 and many former government officials were imprisoned at Sint-Michielsgestel. The administration of the country was largely controlled by Seyss-Inquart himself. He oversaw the politicisaton of cultural groups "right down to the chessplayers' club" through the Kulturkammer and set up a number of other politicised associations. Germany demanded occupation costs in the region of 50 million marks per month.

When the Allies advanced into the Netherlands the Nazi regime enacted a 'scorched earth' policy and destroyed docks and harbours to flood much of the country. The civilian population, with much agricultural land useless and with limited transport that could have moved food stocks for civilian use (partly due to civil disobedience), suffered in almost-famine conditions from September 1944 until early 1945, with around 30,000 Dutch people starving to death. Seyss-Inquart remained Reichskommissar until May 8, 1945, when, after a meeting with Karl Dönitz, he was captured in Hamburg.

Viktor Lutze

Victor Lutze was born in Bevergen, Germany on 28th December, 1890. He joined the German Army in 1912 and fought in the First World War.

After the war Lutz joined the police force. A member of the National Socialist German Workers Party (NSDAP) and the Prussian State Council he was appointed police president of Hanover in 1933.

When Ernst Röhm was murdered during the Night of the Long Knives Lutz became leader of the emasculated Sturm Abteilung (SA).

Lutze remained as police president of Hanover until he was killed in a car crash on the autobahn on 2nd May 1943.

Adolf Hitler and Heinrich Himmler at the 1934 Nuremberg Nazi Party rally with Victor Lutze, head of the SA (Sturmabteilung). Ca. August - September 1934.

Albert Kesselring

Albert Kesselring, the son of school teacher, was born in Bayreuth, Germany, on 8th August, 1881. He joined the German Army in 1904 and became an officer cadet in the 2nd Bavarian Foot Artillery Regiment at Metz.

During the First World War Kesselring was transferred to the German Army Air Service where he trained as a balloon observer. While in this post he developed a close friendship with Hermann Göring.

Kesselring remained in the armed forces and was promoted to major general in 1932. The following year he joined the recently established Luftwaffe where he served under Erhard Milch. In June 1936, despite the objections of Milch, Göring appointed Kesselring as the organization's chief of staff.

On the outbreak of the Second World War Kesselring became commander of 1st Air Fleet and provided air support to General Fedor von Bock and Army Group North in the invasion of Poland. The following year he moved to the 2nd Air Fleet and supported the infantry in the invasions of Belgium, Holland and France. Despite criticisms for his performance during the Dunkirk evacuations, Kesselring was made a field marshal on 19th July 1940.

Kesselring remained in North Africa where he supported General Erwin Rommel in the Desert War. On 10th November 1942 Kesselring was appointed to serve under Benito Mussolini as deputy commander of

Italian forces. In this position he was unable to prevent the loss of Tunisia and Sicily.

In the winter of 1943 Kesselring withdrew his forces to what became known as the Gustav Line on the Italian peninsula south of Rome. Organized along the Garigliano and Rapido rivers it included Monte Cassino, a hilltop site of a sixth-century Benedictine monastery. Defended by 15 German divisions the line was fortified with gun pits, concrete bunkers, turreted machine-gun emplacements, barbed-wire and minefields.

On 25th October 1944 Kesselring was seriously injured when his car collided with a gun coming out of a side road. He was in hospital for three months and his command in Italy was taken over by General Heinrich Vietinghoff. When he recovered Adolf Hitler named Kesselring as supreme commander in the south of the country.

Kesselring, the only one of the early field marshals not to be sacked by Hitler, was taken prisoner on 6th May 1945. Tried as a war criminal he was found guilty on 6th May 1947 and condemned to death. Soon afterwards this sentence was commuted to life in prison and was released for health reasons in October 1952. The following year he published his autobiography, A Soldier to the Last Day (1953). Albert Kesselring died on 16th July 1960.

Robert Ley

Robert Ley (February 15, 1890 - October 25, 1945) was a prominent government figure in Nazi Germany.

He was born in Niederbreidenbach, Germany. He studied at the university of Bonn and received a degree in chemistry. During WW I he was a pilot. Shot down in 1917, he spent two years as a French POW. He worked for IG Farbenindustrie after the war, but was dismissed in 1928.

He joined the NSDAP in 1925 and quickly became a Gauleiter. In 1932 he was elected to the Reichstag and also succeeded Gregor Strasser as head of the Reichsorganisation der NSDAP. In April 1933 Hitler ordered the suppression of the German trade unions and appointed Ley to head the operations.

In early May troops occupied trade union buildings, union funds were confiscated and union leaders were arrested. The unions were replaced with a single organisation, the Deutsche Arbeitsfront (DAF, German Labor Front) which was headed by Ley from May 10, 1933. The Christian trade unions were not reduced in the initial efforts but lasted little more than a month longer.

At the end of WW II Reichsleiter Ley fled to Berchtesgaden but was captured on May 16, 1945 and sent to trial at Nuremberg. But he committed suicide by hanging himself in his cell before the trial proper could begin; "Robert Ley, the field marshal of the battle against labor, answered our indictment with suicide. Apparently he knew no better answer". He had stated, that he could not bear the accusation of being a war criminal.

Robert Ley (1890-1945) German Nazi leader during speech in Berlin Sportpalast.

Carl Oberg

Carl Oberg was born in Hamburg, Germany in 1897. He joined the German Army and served in the First World War. After the war he joined the Freikorps and took part in the Kapp Putsch in 1920.

Oberg worked for a tropical-fruit trading company before enduring a long period of unemployment. In 1930 he acquired a tobacco stand in Hamburg.

Oberg joined the Nazi Party (NSDAP) and in 1932 he went to Munich where he worked with Richard Heydrich. He eventually became Heydrich's right-hand man in the SD Security Service.

In 1938 Oberg was given command of an SS (Schutzstaffel) battalion in Mecklenburg. The following year he became chief of police in Zwickau.

On the outbreak of the Second World War Oberg went to Poland and became SS and Police Leader in the Radom district where he was responsible for rounding up Jews and the drafting of Poles for forced labour.

In March 1942, Oberg was promoted to SS-Brigadeführer and two months later was posted to Paris where he became SS and Police Leader in occupied France. In this position he brought in severe measures to deal with the French Resistance including the shooting of hostages. Oberg was also responsible for applying the Final Solution in France. This action resulted in 75,000 Jews being deported from France to extermination camp in Nazi Germany and Poland.

Oberg was promoted to SS-Obergruppenführer and police general in August 1944. Later that year Oberg was posted to the command of a military unit that was part of an army formation commanded by Heinrich Himmler.

In June 1945 Oberg was arrested by Allied troops. The following year he was extradited to France where he was brought to trial. Convicted of war crimes, Oberg was sentenced to death on 9th October, 1954. After an appeal, this was reduced to life imprisonment.

President Charles De Gaulle granted Oberg a pardon in 1965. Carl Oberg died later that year in Germany.

General Karl Oberg, leader of the SS and Gestapo Chief in Paris, France. He was known as the "Butcher of Paris".

Werner von Blomberg

Werner Blomberg was born in Stargard, Germany, on 2nd September, 1878. He joined the German Army and served as a second lieutenant in the 73rd Fusilier Regiment. He attended the War Academy (1904-07) before joining the General Staff in 1908.

On the outbreak of the First World War Blomberg was General Staff Officer with the 19th Reserve Division. He served on the Western Front where won the Pour le Mérite. By the end of the war he had reached the rank of major. Blomberg's two brothers were both killed in the conflict.

Blomberg remained in the army and in 1920 was promoted to lieutenant colonel and was appointed Chief of Staff of the Döberitz Brigade. Four years later General Hans von Seeckt appointed him as chief of army training.

In 1927 Blomberg was promoted to the rank of major general and was appointed chief of the Troop Office. In this position he clashed with Kurt von Schleicher and in 1929 was sent to East Prussia to serve under Walther von Reichenau.

In 1932 Blomberg was head of the German delegation at the Geneva Disarmament Conference. The following year Adolf Hitler appointed him minister of defence and in 1935 minister of war and commander in chief of the German Army. It was Blomberg's idea to get all soldiers to pledge an oath of personal loyalty to Hitler. In April 1936 Blomberg became Hitler's first field marshal.

Hermann Göring was jealous of Blomberg's power and used the Gestapo to obtain embarrassing information about his private life. In January, 1938, Blomberg resigned when he discovered that Göring was planning to make public the fact that his new young wife was a former prostitute.

After the Second World War Blomberg was captured by Allied troops and gave evidence at the Nuremberg War Crimes Trial. Werner Blomberg died while being held in detention on 14th March, 1946.

JOSEF MENGALE

Dr. Josef Mengele (March 16, 1911–February 7, 1979), also known as the Angel of Death, was a Nazi doctor who performed experiments on prisoners in Auschwitz which were condemned as murderously sadistic and participated in the selections of people to be sent to the gas chambers.

Mengele's nickname was Beppo.

Mengele was the eldest of three sons of Karl Mengele (1881–1959) and his wife Walburga (d.1946), well-to-do Bavarian industrialists.

In 1931, at the age of 20, Mengele joined the Stahlhelm (Steel Helmet); he joined the SA in 1933, and applied for Nazi party membership in 1937. In 1938 he joined the SS, and in 1938–1939 served six months with a specially trained mountain light-infantry regiment. In 1940 he was placed in the reserve medical corps, following which he served three years with a Waffen-SS unit. In 1942 he was wounded at the Russian front and was pronounced medically unfit for combat. Because he had acquitted himself brilliantly in the face of the enemy during the Eastern Campaign, he was promoted to the rank of Captain. Afterward he volunteered to serve at a concentration camp, and he was sent to the death camp Auschwitz and became the chief medical officer of the camp on May 24, 1943.

It was during his 21-month stay at Auschwitz that Dr. Mengele achieved infamy, gaining the nickname "Angel of Death." When rail-cars filled with prisoners arrived in Auschwitz II Birkenau, Mengele would frequently be waiting on the platform to personally select which of them would be retained for work and experimentation and which would be sent immediately to the gas chambers.

Josef Mengele left Auschwitz disguised as a member of the regular German infantry. He turned up at the Gross-Rosen work camp and left well before it was liberated. He was then seen at Matthausen and shortly after he was captured as a POW and held near Munich. He was released by the Allies, who had no idea that he was in their midst. Mengele departed for Argentina in 1949, where many other fleeing Nazi officials had also sought refuge, but moved from country to country afterward to avoid capture. Mengele divorced his wife Irene, and in 1958 married his brother Karl's widow, Martha, and later she and her son moved to Argentina to join Mengele.

Despite international efforts to track him down, he was never apprehended and lived for 35 years hiding under various aliases. He lived in Paraguay and Brazil until his death in 1979, when he suffered a stroke while swimming in the ocean and drowned. He was not tracked down by Nazi hunters until the mid-1980s, and in 1992 DNA tests on his bones confirmed his identity.

Eva Braun

(1912-1945) Hitler's mistress from 1932 and his wife during the last few hours of his life, Eva Braun was born in Munich, the daughter of a school teacher. Of middle-class Catholic background, she first met Hitler in the studio of his photographer friend, Heinrich Hoffmann (q.v.), in 1929, describing him to her sister, Ilse, as "a gentleman of a certain age with a funny moustache and carrying a big felt hat."

At that time Eva Braun still worked for Hoffmann as an office assistant, later becoming a photo laboratory worker, helping to process pictures of Hitler. The blonde, fresh-faced, slim, photographer's assistant was an athletic girl, fond of skiing, mountain climbing and gymnastics as well as dancing.

After the death of Geli Raubal, Hitler's niece, she became his mistress, living in his Munich flat, in spite of the opposition of her father who disliked the association on political and personal grounds. In 1935, after an abortive suicide attempt, Hitler bought her a villa in a Munich suburb, near to his own home, providing her with a Mercedes and a chauffeur for personal use. In his first will of 2 May 1938 he put her at the top of his personal bequests - in the event of his death she was to receive the equivalent of £600 a year for the rest of her life.

In 1936 she moved to Hitler's Berghof at Berchtesgaden where she acted as his hostess. Reserved, indifferent to politics and keeping her distance from most of the Führer's intimates, Eva Braun led a completely isolated life in the Führer's Alpine retreat and later in Berlin. They rarely appeared in public together and few Germans even knew of her existence. Even the Führer's closest associates were not certain of the exact nature of their relationship, since Hitler preferred to avoid suggestions of intimacy and was never wholly relaxed in her company.

Eva Braun spent most of her time exercising, brooding, reading cheap novelettes, watching romantic films or concerning herself with her own appearance. Her loyalty to Hitler never flagged. After he survived the July 1944 plot she wrote Hitler an emotional letter, ending: "From our first meeting I swore to follow you anywhere--even unto death--I live only for your love."

In April 1945 she joined Hitler in the Führerbunker, as the Russians closed in on Berlin. She declined to leave in spite of his orders, claiming to others that she was the only person still loyal to him to the bitter end. "Better that ten thousand others die than he be lost to Germany," she would constantly repeat to friends.

On 29 April 1945 Hitler and Eva Braun were finally married. The next day she committed suicide by swallowing poison, two minutes before Hitler took his own life. On Hitler's orders, both bodies were cremated with petrol in the Reich Chancellery garden above the bunker. Her charred corpse was later discovered by the Russians.

Opening ceremony for the 1935 Nuremberg Rally. The front row (from left to right) is composed of: Himmler, Lutze, Hitler, Hess and Streicher.

New Year reception for the Diplomatic Corps, 1934.

Since it was always Adolf Hitler's intention to go to war, he knew that a major rearmament process had to be undertaken before his forces could take on the might of the Allies. Germany was, however, bound by the terms of the Versailles Treaty, and this expressly forbid any such rearmament. Ever since the end of World War I, Hitler had been making use of the resentment felt by the vast majority of the German people towards the settlement terms of the peace treaty. In order to rally popular support and to test the resolve of the Allies, he once again played the unfairness card by announcing that Germany would withdraw from the League of Nations. His excuse was that the other European nations did not permit Germany equality in armaments. His propaganda machine had generated enough support for him to be able to afford to go to the people in a plebiscite, and his estimation of the mood was justified when 95.1percent of the electorate backed his decision.

In 1935, Hitler further risked foreign aggression when he announced that Germany was going to rearm with the creation of a peacetime army of 36 divisions. This clearly violated the terms of the Treaty of Versailles, and the allies met to form a new pact against the fresh threat from Germany. The meeting was held in the town of Stresa, in Italy, and the agreement became known as the Stresa Front. To back this up, several other pacts were initiated. France did a deal with the Soviet Union, which then in turn signed a pact with Czechoslovakia. Hitler knew, however, that he would be able to turn the various countries against each other when the time came. He started by doing a deal with Britain over limits to the size of the German navy. The

Official photograph for the state visit by Julius Gömbös, Prime Minister of Hungary.

Hitler after the New Year reception for the Diplomatic Corps, 1934.

deal that was finally struck was in clear breech of the Treaty of Versailles, which angered both France and Italy—Hitler, however, was delighted.

Hitler's plan to weaken the Stresa Front had worked, and he hoped that this would mean he would be able to get away with reclaiming the Rhineland. If he did so, it would not only violate the Treaty of Versailles, but also the Locarno Pact, in which the Germans agreed to comply with the demilitarisation of the Rhineland. Hitler knew that the Allies wanted to avoid going to war, but he also knew that his forces were not strong enough to fight them. In March 1936, he followed his instincts … troops in to the Rhin… to stave off any reprisals …, Hitler offered non-ag… o France and Belgium, … hat Germany would rejoi… Nations. To his great … merely made verbal c… and did nothing mor…

As part of the rear… s, Hitler tested his troo… amount of new milita… that had been secretly … supporting the Natio… Spanish Civil War. Th… y 1937, and as far as th… concerned, also serve… reactions of the allies. … fit was that Germany was joined in the effort by Italy—this further weakened the Stresa Front, but once again, the Allies demonstrated a 'do nothing' policy, an attitude that was to have serious repercussions in the very near future. The fact that German troops were exposed to action on the Iberian Peninsula was very significant—it acted as a glorified military exercise, and allowed them to hone large numbers of raw recruits into well-practised soldiers. The Spanish Civil War ended in 1939, with victory going to the Nationalists, led by Franco—thanks in part to German and Italian support.

During rearmament, Germany did its best to align itself with as many potential allies as possible. In November 1936, it signed the first part of the Anti-Comintern Pact with Japan. The Comintern or Communist International was an international association of national communist parties which was originally founded in 1919. Its stated aim was to foster world revolution, but in reality it was an organisation that allowed the Soviet Union to exert control over the international communist movement. In 1937, the pact was extended to include Italy; the right-wing regimes in Germany and Italy had much in common, and in late 1937 the two countries also signed the Rome-Berlin Axis Treaty.

At this time Hitler was not only busy dealing with foreign affairs—he had tired of sharing power with the remaining conservatives, and in February 1938, replaced Foreign Minister von Neurath as well as the other leading conservatives—this left the Nazis in complete political control. The next part of Hitler's personal agenda was to ensure that the military would follow his orders as he stepped up pressure on the allies with his territorial demands. To do this he used dirty stories dragged up by Heydrich as excuses to sack Blomberg and Fritsch who were the two top commanders of the armed forces, and took over personal command of the military.

With the Rhineland reclaimed,

Hitler and Reich Foreign Minister von Neurath.

Hitler and Mussolini in Venice, 1934.

and full control of the army under his belt, Hitler decided that the time had come to annex Austria. Although the Nazi Party was banned in Austria, they enjoyed much popular support there. The man who brought in the ban was the previous Chancellor, a man called Engelbert Dollfuss—in retaliation, the Nazis had murdered him in 1934. His replacement Chancellor Kurt von Schuschnigg did not like or trust Hitler either, and in an attempt to smooth the waters, Hitler sent his predecessor Franz von Papen to act as his ambassador. Matters improved when an agreement was reached in which Germany recognised Austria's sovereignty and in return Austria would acknowledge itself as a 'German State' and 17,000 Nazis would be released from her prisons.

Hitler then tried intimidating Chancellor Schuschnigg into reinstating all the Nazi politicians that he had removed from the government, and installing Nazi Artur von Seyss-Inquart as Minister of the Interior. He was given just three days to accede to Hitler's demands, which eventually he agreed to, more out of appeasement than anything else. He was, however, disturbed to hear that Hitler had given a speech in the Reichstag, saying that he was not going to recognise Austria's sovereignty after all, and that Germany was responsible for all the German citizens currently in Austria. Schuschnigg decided to put the matter before the people, and set March 13 for a referendum—this was simply going to ask 'Are you in favour of a free and German, independent and social, Christian and united Austria?'.

While this would appear to be a fair way for the people to show their opinions on the matter, Hitler was not interested in such niceties. When he heard about Schuschnigg's plans, he flew into a rage and ordered his troops into Austria—agreement or no agreement. This sudden annexation became known as the Anschluss. When the troops of the German Eighth Army arrived on the morning of March 12th, they received a massive welcome, with vast crowds cheering and shouting. Hitler himself arrived shortly afterwards, and when he reached his home ground at Linz, he was cheered by over 100,000 people. When a new referendum was held on April 10th to ask for the people's opinion on Austria's unification with the German Reich, the vote was officially given as being 99.75percent in favour.

Once again the allies stood by and did nothing—their own domestic problems were taking priority over foreign affairs, which only served to whet Hitler's appetite for more. In September 1938, Neville Chamberlain—the British prime minister, went to Adolf Hitler's home in Berchtesgaden to discuss German demands for the Sudetenland. Hitler stated that unless the allies acceded to his demands, Germany would invade Czechoslovakia. This resulted in crisis meetings with the French and Czechs, after which Hitler was told that his proposals were unacceptable. He met with Chamberlain again, and told him that all Czech troops, police officers, and administrative officials had to leave the area straight away. On top of this was a long list of other demands, including that Czechoslovakia must hand over more territories to Poland and Hungary; the deadline was October 1st.

Hitler signs papers in the Chancellery; with him is Viktor Lutze who became chief of staff of the SA after Röhm's assassination.

Hitler and the French ambassador, André François-Poncet.

Hitler at the New Year reception for the Diplomatic Corps, 1934.

Hitler with the Polish Foreign Minister Colonel Beck.

Hitler confers with his press chief, Dr. Otto Dietrich.

Anthony Eden and Sir John Simon (British Foreign Minister) discuss German rearmament with Hitler, von Neurath and von Ribbentrop. The result of the talks was the Anglo-German Naval Treaty of June 1935.

Hitler signs the Munich Agreement.

Hitler knew that Britain and France were unlikely to go to war on their own over territorial demands for parts of Czechoslovakia, however, he was conscious that if they allied with the Soviet Union, it would be very bad news for Germany. On Mussolini's suggestion, a conference was held in Munich where representatives from Germany, Britain, France and Italy discussed the current situation. By holding the meeting on German soil, Hitler was able to ensure that neither Czechoslovakia nor the Soviet Union would be present—this minimised the risk of a pact between the allies and the Soviets. He also managed to allay fears of further territorial expansion by promising that this would be the last demand he would make. Both Britain's Neville Chamberlain and France's Edouard Daladier were desperate to avoid war, and used Hitler's promises of future non-aggression as an excuse to hand over the Sudetenland. The transferral, which became known as the Munich Agreement, infuriated the Czechs, but they were bluntly told that Britain would not go to war over the Sudetenland.

This act of appeasement pleased those who believed Hitler's promises that he wouldn't make any further territorial claims, since it seemed a new European war had been avoided. Hitler, however, had other ideas. When the German troops arrived in the Sudetenland, they were greeted by cheering crowds, but not everyone was happy to see them on Czech soil. Emil Hacha was installed as the new president after the previous one resigned, but in March 1939, not long after he took power, Hitler told him at a meeting that German troops would

Neville Chamberlain returns to England waving a piece of paper that he thought meant, 'Peace in our time.' As we know, it didn't.

Preparations for war—1: The 1935 Nuremberg Rally saw an expression of Germany's refound military might. These photographs show anti-aircraft teams ranging in on Luftwaffe aircraft overhead. The Luftwaffe would play a major part in Wehrmacht early war successes.

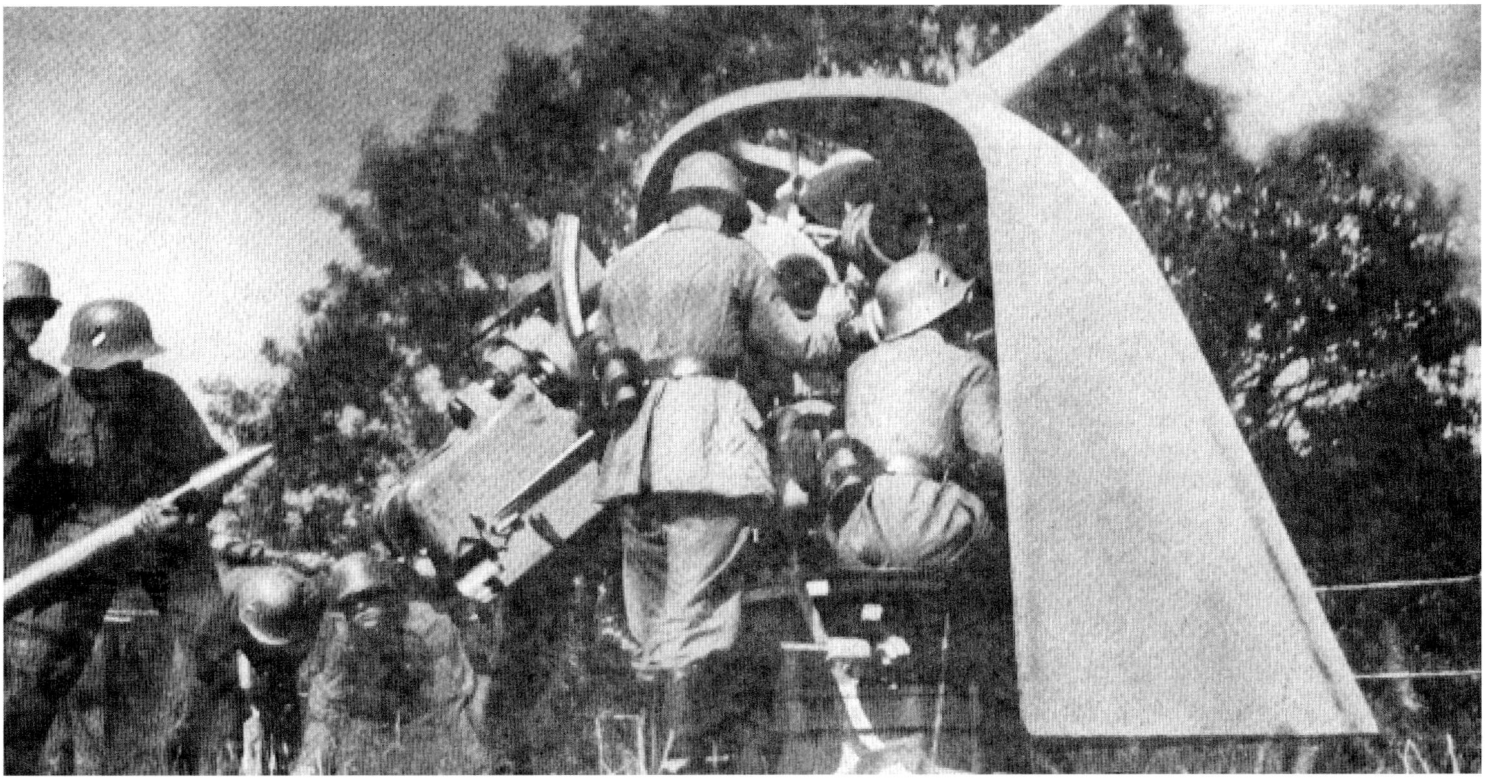

Preparations for war—2: German naval power was scuttled at Scapa Flow at the end of World War I. In the 1930s she tried to revive her navy (the lower photograph shows the launch of the Admiral Graf Spee*) and coastal defences. But it would be Kriegsmarine U-boats that proved the most effective German naval force.*

Hitler visiting the fleet.

march into Czechoslovakia at 6am the following morning. He was given a stark choice—either tell the Czech army not to resist, or the country would be destroyed. Under much duress, Hacha gave in and the next day silent crowds watched the German invaders march in.

With the German invasion of Czechoslovakia in March 1939, however, it became obvious to even the most naïve that the Nazis were now intent on further territorial conquests. The new target was Poland, and once again Hitler sought a pretext for an invasion. In this case he used a strip of land called the Polish Corridor as his excuse—this was a region which separated Germany from East Prussia which had been given to Poland after World War I. Hitler demanded that the port of Danzig—which was within the corridor, return to German ownership. This time, however, the Allies realised that appeasement was no longer an option, and Poland flatly refused to give Danzig up. As Hitler prepared his forces for an invasion, Neville Chamberlain declared that Britain and France would go to the aid of Poland if Germany should attack. When Hitler heard this he declared, 'I'll cook a stew that they'll choke on!'.

Wehrmacht Day at the Nuremberg Rally of 1935.

Hitler knew that he could not simultaneously fight a war with the Soviets as well as the Allies, even though he had every intention of invading Russia. He blamed the Soviets for colluding with the Jews to bring down Germany, and so wanted to end the Bolshevik regime. To buy some time, he arranged a non-aggression pact between Germany and Russia—this basically stated that after Poland had been invaded, Stalin and Hitler would divide the country up between them. Russia would also gain the Baltic states of Latvia and Estonia. The deal which was known as either the Nazi-Soviet Pact or the Molotov-Ribbentrop Pact was signed on August 23, 1939.

Hitler once again used his security services to create a suitable excuse to send troops into Poland. The ingenious Heydrich had some of his SS officers disguise themselves as Polish soldiers—they then attacked a German radio station in Gleiwicz. These soldiers then announced on live radio that Poland was invading Germany, and Hitler suddenly had his pretext for invasion. German troops invaded Poland on September 1st 1939, and after Hitler rejected demands to withdraw, Britain and France declared war on Germany on September 3, 1939—World War II had begun.

Above and Above Right: In March 1935 Hitler repudiated the terms of the Treaty of Versailles, announcing that he would build an army of half a million men. This is the parade that celebrated Germany's rearmament.

Left: German Junkers Ju52 aircraft over Nuremberg. The Ju52 would be the Luftwaffe's transport workhorse during World War II.

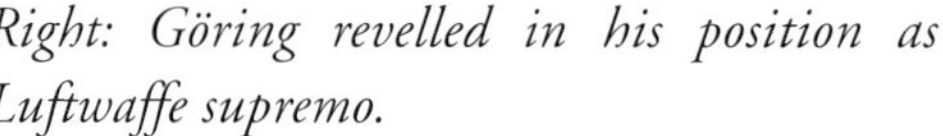

Right: Göring revelled in his position as Luftwaffe supremo.

Left: March 7, 1936, and German troops march into the demilitarised Rhineland over the bridge at Mainz.

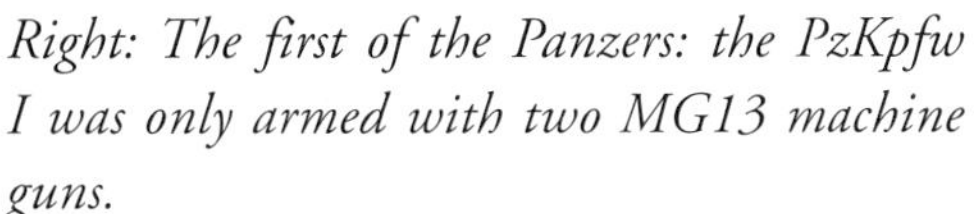

Right: The first of the Panzers: the PzKpfw I was only armed with two MG13 machine guns.

The business end of the Admiral Scheer. *She carried two three-gun turrets armed with 11-inch guns and had a secondary armament of eight 5.9-inch, six 4.1-inch AA and eight 3-pdr AA guns.*

Naval march-past on Wehrmacht Day at the 1935 Nuremberg Rally.

War

Poland

When Germany invaded Poland on September 1, 1939, it signalled the start of the largest military conflict in history. Two days later, Britain and France declared war on Germany. If Germany's continued invasion from the west wasn't bad enough for the Polish people, three weeks later Russia joined the conflict and sent armies into the country from the east. Poland could not withstand such an onslaught, and by the end of the month only Warsaw still held out. Much of the country lay in ruins, and on October 6, the capital city also fell.

German troops stream into Poland spearheaded by armoured forces. The first Blitzkrieg (lighting war) attack of World War II started at 0445 hours on September 1, 1939. By October 3 Polish resistance had been overcome.

German occupation of the Norwegian capital, Oslo, followed the surrender of the city on April 9, 1940.

German cycle patrol takes cover during the Norwegian campaign.

Scandinavia

With the fall of Poland, Hitler looked to the next stages of his territorial expansion—he postponed an attack westwards since copies of his invasion plans had fallen into Allied hands. In the meantime, he drove north. Scandinavia was of great strategic value—not only did Sweden provide much of Germany's iron ore, but Norway's geographical positioning was of vital significance for naval control of the North Sea. Hitler knew that he only had so much time before things would get much more difficult for him in Scandinavia, for trouble was brewing over the waters in Britain.

To complicate matters, Stalin's troops invaded Finland on November 30, 1939, and the Allies intended to send a force to help the Finns defend themselves. This would have put Allied troops in a position where they could threaten Germany's iron ore supply, however, before this could happen a peace settlement was signed between Russia and Finland. In order to make sure that he had control of Norwegian naval bases, Hitler decided to invade Norway. He assembled a force of 100,000 troops, 71 ships, and 28 submarines for the surprise attack which he named the Weserübung (Weser Exercise). Although taking Norway was his main objective, Hitler decided to take Denmark at the same time. His forces began the invasion on April 9th 1940, and he described the action as 'the boldest and most impudent in the history of warfare'.

Denmark was over-run within two hours, for her forces were too small to stave off the heavy units of the German army and air force; the Danes had no choice but to agree to an unconditional surrender. The Germans issued an ultimatum to the Norwegians, but the king refused to surrender. After several weeks of fierce fighting the lightly-armed Norwegian army (backed by small numbers of Allied troops) was beaten, and in mid-June 1940 Norway capitulated.

German troops disembark in the first amphibious landings of the war in April 1940. To all intents Norway would fall within the month.

German supply column crosses a hastily repaired bridge in Norway.

Scenes from the Norway campaign. German troops in action (above); note the MG34 with its magazine attached. The lower photo shows Junkers Ju87 Stuka crews relaxing on Stavanger airport which was targeted for capture by the first parachute operation of the war.

THE ATTACK ON THE WEST

Once Hitler was satisfied that his northern and eastern borders were under control, he started on the western front. Even though Britain and France had declared war on Germany, they failed to act while the Polish invasion was going on, when Germany would have been at her most vulnerable. In the west it became known as the 'phoney war', while the Germans called it the Sitzkrieg (Sitting War). Realising that the Allies were less prepared for war then he had thought, Hitler decided to launch an invasion force westwards, with the initial targets being Luxembourg, Belgium, Holland, and France.

Hitler knew that the Allied politicians would take time to react, therefore if his attack was going to be relatively unopposed it would have to be completed very quickly. Hitler also intended to out-manoeuvre any possible mutual support agreements by invading Holland and Belgium first. Both countries were neutral, and it would take a significant amount of time for the Allies to try to persuade them to sign up to a pact against Germany. If his armies could over-run them fast enough, it would prevent any such threat. Hitler also had to keep an eye on Stalin, however, since he knew that Russia would move in from the east if Germany got too tied up in the west.

Realising that time was of the essence, Hitler acted, and without waiting for matters to be completed in Norway, on May 10, 1940, German armies invaded the Netherlands, Belgium and Luxembourg. Two days

Belgian troops on manoeuvres. In May 1940, overwhelmed by the German forces that had invaded the neutral kingdom, King Leopold ordered the surrender of the Belgian Army.

German Fallschirmjäger *(paratroops) spearheaded the Blitzkrieg campaign into Holland.*

later they also attacked France, but instead of coming through Belgium and northern France as they had done in the first war, their main thrust was through the Ardennes. This was a hilly and forested area that was considered by most to be completely unsuitable for armoured military units to operate in. The plan, which was devised by General Erich von Manstein, took everyone by surprise. While they did send 29 divisions into Belgium, this was a diversionary attack, and it drew all the Allied forces towards it. The main force, however, which was comprised of 40 divisions came through further south; the French were totally unprepared for this manoeuvre, and their forces in the region collapsed.

Meanwhile the combined efforts of the British Expeditionary Force and the main units of the French army were totally overwhelmed as they tried to defend Belgium. The German tanks fought in close columns supported from the air by Stuka dive-bombers—an extremely effective form of warfare which became known as Blitzkrieg (lightning war). The Allied armies had never faced such tactics before, and they were not equipped to deal with such an onslaught. Indeed, most of their military hardware was left over from World War I, and was totally outclassed by the modern weapons of the Wehrmacht.

On the same day that Germany attacked France, Winston Churchill replaced Neville Chamberlain as the British Prime Minister. This marked a sea change in the Allies political attitude—instead of appeasement, from this point forward there would be a tough military stance. The Low Countries were even less able to defend

The years of militarism since 1933 had welded the German forces into a superb fighting unit that completely routed the western allies. This is a photo from the 1935 Nuremberg Rally.

themselves than the Allied forces—Luxembourg capitulated in one day, and Holland capitulated in five days.

The German armies that had advanced through the Ardennes then worked their way north towards the

The long lines of British and French troops queuing for evacuation at Dunkirk. Remarkably nearly 340,000 were saved to fight again.

main Allied forces. This resulted in the Belgian army, nine divisions of the British Expeditionary Force, and ten divisions of the French First Army being pinned against the coast at Dunkirk, on the shores of the English Channel. Hitler particularly wanted to capture the Channel coast because he thought that if his armies could secure the naval bases there, they could mount a naval blockade of the British Isles.

For some reason, however, Hitler called his troops to halt their advances. Instead of moving in and finishing off the Allies, he called his tanks back. There are many theories as to why he did this. It is said that he wanted the Luftwaffe to finish the job, as the marshy ground near the coast was unsuitable for tank warfare. Another theory is that he wanted to give the British a chance to withdraw gracefully so that he could broker a peace deal with them. A third possibility is that his armies had moved so quickly that the support columns could not keep up, and they simply ran out of fuel. The most likely explanation is that all these issues had a bearing on Hitler's decision. Whatever the factors were, it gave the British the chance to mount the most incredible rescue mission in history.

The evacuation of Dunkirk was accomplished by a combination of factors—the Royal Air Force staged a frantic series of attacks against the Luftwaffe. This, together with bad weather significantly reduced the effectiveness of the German air onslaught. When Hitler realised that the Luftwaffe was not able to do the job on its own, he ordered the tanks to move forward once again. Meanwhile as 40,000 French troops did their best to hold out against the Germans, an evacuation fleet of 850 vessels—boats and ships of all sizes, crossed the channel & rescued a total of 338,226 Allied troops.

Although a massive amount of Allied equipment was abandoned at Dunkirk, it was a mixed blessing - whilst it meant that the troops had few weapons left, it rid the British army of most of its outdated hardware. Consequently, when the rearmament process began, most of the equipment was brand new and of the latest designs. Once the Allies had left, France could no longer hold back the advancing German forces. Her armies collapsed, and the French asked for an armistice on June 17. Hitler was ecstatic—Belgium had already surrendered on May 27, and his advances westward had been a complete success. He installed Marshal Phillippe Petain in the south of France as a puppet governor, and took direct control of the rest of the country.

A London fireman gazes out across the devastation caused by Luftwaffe bombing in the docklands area of East London. Ruined warehousing can be seen in the background.

The Battle of Britain

With much of mainland Europe under Nazi control, Hitler started the next phase—the invasion of Britain. On paper this should not have presented a significant problem—only the relatively narrow English Channel separated his forces from the shores of southern England. Britain also stood alone, her allies all having fallen to the might of the German armies. Having only just come out of a major economic crisis, America wanted to stay out of the war.

Hitler was in two minds as to how he should go about dealing with Britain. On the one hand, he admired the British—especially the way such a small country had successfully administered its massive colonies for so many years. In many ways this was a role model for his own plans for the Third Reich. With this in mind, he would have rather brokered a peace deal than undertake a military take-over of Britain. On the other hand, he knew that if a pact could not be established, he would have to invade, since Britain and her powerful navies dominated the seas of Western Europe. Herman Göring assured Hitler that his Luftwaffe would soften the British up sufficiently for the invasion to be a forgone conclusion.

Although Hitler was making the necessary arrangements to invade Britain, he was being distracted by what was potentially a far bigger problem—that of Josef Stalin and Russian territorial desires. In the short term, Stalin wanted Romania, but Hitler realised that this was just the tip of the iceberg, and the only solution was the invasion of Russia. This is what he had intended all along, but events were moving faster than he had anticipated, hence in July 1940, he moved the plan forward. Hitler's generals knew that their armies could not cope with the Russian winter, and so they finally managed to persuade him that matters should be put back until the following spring. This left him enough time to deal with Britain.

The aftermath of a Luftwaffe raid on a residential district of the West End of London, April 18, 1941. More than two million British homes were destroyed or damaged by German bombing between September 1940 and May 1941, 60% in London.

Having been used to dealing with the naïve Neville Chamberlain, Hitler had a rude shock when he tried doing business with Winston Churchill. Under his leadership, England would not do any kind of peace deal, and would fight to the bitter end. Hitler could not understand Churchill's attitude, and in July 1940, when it became clear that there was going to be no back-tracking, Hitler ordered an invasion—it was to be launched in September, and codenamed Operation 'Sea Lion'. Although Hitler was confident, his generals were less so. Moving large numbers of troops across the channel would be tough enough, but if they attempted to do so against the full might of the British navy, it would be unthinkable.

Heinkel He111 crew captured after a forced landing.

A double-decker bus lies in a bomb crater after a German air raid on South London, October 10, 1940.

King George VI and Queen Elizabeth touring bombed districts in northwest London, September 1940. Their presence in the capital did much to bolster morale and accounts in part for the esteem with which Queen Elizabeth, the Queen Mother was held throughout her life.

Evacuation of children from the capital started as early as September 1939. Some 3.5 million women and children were sent away from London.

Classic view of to Dornier Do217 bombers over Silvertown—the distinctive oval of the West Ham speedway stadium in Canning Town providing a point of reference.

This Heinkel He111, seen during a bombing raid on July 9, 1940, is flying over the Thames and docks at Wapping—the site of modern London's Canary Wharf development.

The Messerschmitt Bf109 was the best German escort fighter during the Battle of Britain—better than the British Hurricanes and a match for the Spitfire.

Royal Air Force Spitfires patrol the coast of Britain, May 1941.

The attentions of the Royal Air Force would make matters worse, and so the generals argued, a lot of work would need to be done to reduce the effectiveness of both British air and sea power before a crossing of the channel could be achieved. The generals asked Hitler for the invasion to be postponed until the following spring, but this was when he intended to attack Russia, so it was out of the question. Instead, he ordered that the Battle of Britain would take place—this would entail the Luftwaffe destroying as many of the British air and naval bases as possible, along with aircraft, ships, storage depots and any other relevant targets. If this plan worked, then the invasion would take place in September, as originally planned, if not, it would be pushed back until spring.

Although the Royal Air Force were heavily outnumbered, with the secret development of radar, they had a technical advantage. Having early warning of the approach of German aircraft meant that the British could use their small numbers of fighter planes extremely effectively. They took an enormous toll of German fighters and bombers, but by the end of August, Luftwaffe Chief Hermann Göring realised that he needed to focus his forces on the destruction of the RAF before they could go back to their other targets. The RAF could not hold out against the entire might of the Luftwaffe, and they were in real trouble. It was only when German planes accidentally bombed some civilian homes in London, that things changed. In retaliation, British planes bombed Berlin the next night, and this so angered Hitler that the Luftwaffe was ordered to switch their attentions from attacking the RAF to the wholesale bombing of British cities. This unexpected respite allowed the RAF to rebuild itself, and having failed to take control of British airspace, on September 17, Hitler postponed Operation 'Sea Lion'.

Above and Above right: The war at sea—in coastal waters and seas within range, land-based aircraft played a significant role in the war at sea. These two photographs show a German aircraft in the process of bombing a British coastal vessel.

British ships in the Mediterranean; the lead vessel is laying smoke while the second prepares a salvo of 5.25-inch guns.

As in the first war, the strategy of the British naval forces was to blockade German surface ships. The German battleship Bismarck tried to run the blockade and in the process destroyed the battlecruiser HMS Hood. In the end, the Royal Navy had too many ships and Bismarck herself was hunted down and sunk.

The War at Sea

Russia and the Balkans

In the autumn of 1940, Hitler was facing a serious dilemma—although he wanted to invade Russia, he was not ready to do so. Stalin, however, was trying to acquire the Romanian oilfields, however, these were a vital component of the German war effort. In 1939, Romania had agreed to export most of its oil to Germany, and Hitler could not afford to lose this supply. For now the invasion of England could wait—Romania was far more important. Hitler needed to keep his plans for the invasion of Russia secret—they could only work with the element of surprise, and so he could not be too overtly aggressive with Stalin.

After much political wrangling, Hitler stood by and allowed Stalin to take several Romanian territories. Shortly after this Bulgaria and Hungary also demanded parts of Romania, and Hitler brokered a deal whereby sufficient lands were handed over. To guarantee Romania's future security, he signed a protection guarantee, whereby Germany and Italy would ensure her borders. This gave Hitler just what he wanted—a legitimate reason to defend the Romanian oilfields against all comers. Stalin was furious, and the situation between the two leaders started to deteriorate. Bitter arguments over Finland and Romania followed, and in December 1940, Hitler changed the code name for the invasion of Russia to Operation 'Barbarossa', with the invasion still set for the following spring.

Matters quickly got out of control for Hitler, however. Jealous of all Germany's military successes, Mussolini wanted some of the action for Italy. Further to this, he wanted to pay Hitler back for never telling him in advance about any of his plans. The ideal opportunity as far as Mussolini was concerned would be an invasion of Greece. He set the date for October 28, 1940, and the attack went ahead as planned. Mussolini, however, had underestimated his opponents, and the Greeks with Allied help fought his troops back. Hitler was furious about not being told in advance, but had little option but to reinforce the Italian

A torpedoed tanker in the Atlantic, 1942.

The Battle of the Atlantic was pivotal to the survival of Britain. Here the corvette HMS Dianthus picks up survivors from a U-boat sunk by HMS *Assiniboine*.

British motor torpedo boat on trials in 1939.

A U.S. Coast Guard cutter fires depth charges. After America's entry into the war, the wolfpacks became the hunted as well as the hunter.

Another merchantman sinks: in 1942 1,664 Allied ships were lost, 1,160 to U-boats.

U.S. seamen on leave in London—Allied anti-submarine warfare improved dramatically once the U.S. shipping industry transformed the number of escorts available to convoys.

Coastal patrols required careful lookout for aircraft and German E-boats.

operation—the last thing he needed was an Allied presence near the Romanian oilfields.

By now the winter of 1940 had arrived, and German forces would have to wait until spring before they could operate in the Balkans. This meant that they had little time before Operation 'Barbarossa' would start. To mount an invasion of Greece, German forces would have to cross the Balkans, a region which had a history of complicated politics. Hitler either had to negotiate passage through Hungary, Rumania, and Bulgaria, or his armies could take the direct route through Yugoslavia, which would be the best route from a military stance. This would be very difficult to arrange, however, as not only was there strong anti-Nazi feeling there, but the British were desperately trying to persuade them to resist German pressure.

After much political effort, Hitler managed to create the Tripartite Pact, in which Yugoslavia would be given the Greek port of Salonika, no territory would be ceded to Germany, and no German troops would travel through the country. This was signed by Prince Paul of Yugoslavia on March 24, 1940, however, the Serbians staged a massive revolt, and the Prince was forced to resign. The hard-won pact collapsed, and Hitler raged that the country must be destroyed. He was now at war with Greece and Yugoslavia—on April 6, 1940, German armies invaded both countries simultaneously. Yugoslavia capitulated on April 17 and the Greek mainland capitulated on April 23.

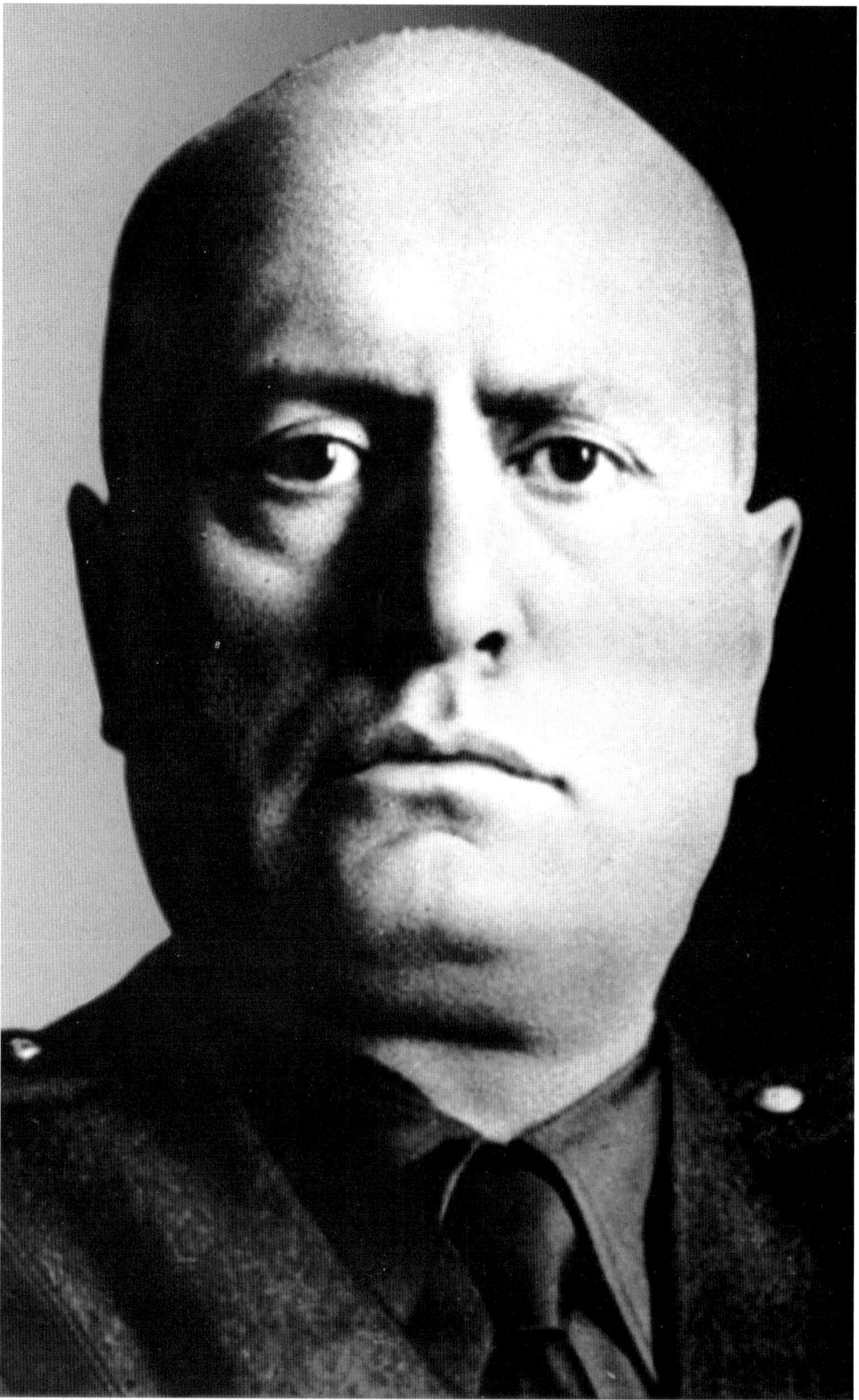

Mussolini was a difficult ally for Hitler: his invasion of Greece put back Operation 'Barbarossa' and contributed to its failure.

British soldiers captured in Greece are marched to a prisoner of war camp. The Germans captured 10,000 Britons, 90,000 Yugoslavs and 270,000 Greeks in their Balkan campaign of March-April 1941.

Operation 'Barbarossa'

Even though the military operations in the Balkans had been successful, they had cost Hitler valuable time. Since his dealings with the Russians were getting steadily worse, he could not afford to wait for spring the next year to launch Operation 'Barbarossa', and so on June 22, 1941, he sent his armies into Russia. It was the largest battle in modern history, with over three million men, more than 7,000 artillery pieces, 3,300 tanks, 600,000 vehicles, 2,770 airplanes, and 625 horses. Hitler thought that with an army of this size, he could win the war in just ten weeks.

Incredibly, Stalin was taken completely by surprise—both Franklin Roosevelt and Winston Churchill had tried to warn him of the impending German invasion, but his suspicious nature led him to believe it was an Allied ruse to break up the Russo-German Pact. At first the Germans made massive territorial gains—on the first day, three Russian infantry divisions were wiped out and another five were all but destroyed. The Luftwaffe destroyed 2,000 Russian planes, many of which were still on the ground, and the Red Army's communications system was disrupted beyond use.

What Hitler had not realised, however, was that even though he was unprepared, Stalin had Russia's ultimate defence on his side—sheer land mass. He could afford to give away massive areas at little cost to himself. The German armies, however, could not possibly hope to take full control of these areas and supply them at the same time. There were very few paved roads in Russia, and so the heavily mechanised German army was at the mercy of the weather; one spell of rain would turn the entire region into a mud-bath. The vast forests and marshes also disoriented the Germans, who found it hard to cope with the enormous scale of the land they were trying to conquer.

Russia also had a population which was more than twice that of Germany, and Stalin was ruthless in his use of manpower, both on the battlefield and in the construction of defence lines.

On June 22, 1941, the Germans attacked Russia—three months later than planned. Immediate successes saw the German forces reach the outskirts of Moscow.

The German six-tube Nebelwerfer (mist or smoke thrower) was introduced in 1942. It was effective against infantry and its distinctive noise provided its nickname, the 'moaning Minnie'.

In the first months of the war on the Eastern Front German troops reached Moscow, but the winter set in and they would never reach so far again.

A man armed with Molotov cocktails attacks a German tank. Undoubtedly a posed photograph, nevertheless the pugnacity of the Russian defences surprised the Germans.

The Russians were also a very tough people, used to a peasant life of toil and hardship. Vitally, however, they were also used to the harsh weather of the bleak Soviet terrain.

Hitler had not thought his plan through properly—in his haste to get back at Stalin he had not considered what would happen if his troops had to cope with the Russian winter. He sent in three army groups—the North, which was the smallest, was composed of 31 divisions. Its task was to go through the Baltic States of Latvia, Estonia, and Lithuania, and move towards Leningrad. The Centre Group, which at 57 divisions was the largest, would attack through Belo-Russia and move on to Smolensk. The South Group, which consisted of 48 divisions, was divided into two sections—North and South. The northern section would invade the Ukraine, and later the Southern section would move into the

Russian troops advance on surrendering Germans.

Germans captured in the battles around Moscow.

The Russian counterattacked again north of Moscow and made immediate gains. On January 16, 1942 German Field Marshal von Leeb became the third of the original three army group commanders to be relieved of command for requesting permission to retreat.

From the start of Barbarossa the Germans were surprised at the effectiveness of the Russian armour. Here a KV-1 heavy tank leads Russian infantry into battle.

Fighting around Sebastopol: Russian Marine units are landed by submarine.

Kharkov saw important battles in 1942 and 1943. Here, in spring 1941, Russian forces are on the advance. A counterattack by von Paulus's Sixth Army will open the Donets corridor to Stalingrad and the crucial battle of the Eastern Front.

At Stalingrad, Russian forces captured 94,000 men of von Paulus's Sixth Army—but 200,000 had already been lost. The scale of the defeat was monumental and from then on German forces on the Eastern Front would be on the retreat.

German flamethrower in action.

Russian troops enter Königsberg in East Prussia.

Ukraine through Romania. As these armies moved through Soviet territory, they were followed up by units of the Einsatzgruppen—these were the special SS death squads which were tasked with identifying and murdering prominent communists and Jews.

Hitler and his generals argued over how the armies should proceed. The impending Russian winter meant that the military wanted to take Moscow so that their armies would have a secure base in which to wait out until spring. Since it was the capital city, it also had major importance as a communications and armaments production centre. On top of this, most of the Russian transport systems ran through Moscow—control of the city would be a major disruption to Russian logistics. Hitler, however, thought that capturing the oil and coal fields in southern Russia was more important.

The Germans continued to win battle after battle—when they captured Kiev in mid-September, they took 665,212 Russian prisoners, 3,718 artillery pieces and 884 tanks. This was the biggest military defeat in history. Hitler then changed his mind and sent his armies to take Moscow, a push he named Operation 'Typhoon'. For this he assembled a massive number of tanks, and before long 650,000 Russian prisoners were taken, along with 5,000 guns, and 1,200 tanks. They made it to within 40 miles of Moscow before Stalin launched his secret weapon—his Siberian ski troops, who numbered 40 divisions of fresh reserve soldiers. As the raging winter turned the countryside to a frozen waste, these fierce troops backed up by large numbers of tanks made the German soldiers life a living hell.

Since Hitler refused to accept that his troops may not take Moscow before winter set in, his army only had summer clothing. In the torrential pre-winter rains, the German army had come to a halt as their vehicles sank in the mud—now, as temperatures fell, their tanks froze up. The sick and wounded were doomed—even healthy men froze to death. In the order of one million German soldiers were killed by the Russians, and a further half million died of cold and sickness.

In their attempt to take and hold Stalingrad, the German army lost 250,000 troops—it became known as the 'mass grave of the Wehrmacht' and the 'Cauldron'. Not long after they gained control of the city, a massive Russian counter-attack encircled them. Desperate to not to withdraw, Hitler tried to keep his armies supplied by air, but this was doomed to failure—there were simply too many troops and too many vehicles for this to work. The German armies had been beaten by a combination of the Russian geography and weather—the scale of which Hitler had never really fully understood when he first contemplated Operation 'Barbarossa'. The war on the eastern front was now a matter of attrition rather than conquest—although both sides made gains and losses here and there, Germany could not possibly compete with Russia when it came to sheer manpower and military hardware.

In 1943 the German commander at Stalingrad surrendered, and the Red Army started a push towards Berlin and final victory. In April 1944, the Polish mounted an armed revolt in the Warsaw Ghetto, but after a couple of weeks of furious fighting, Hitler ordered the ghetto to be completely destroyed. Three months later Polish partisans revolted again—they hoped to be helped by the nearby Russian army, but the Soviets deliberately stood by until the Poles had been annihilated. When the Red Army finally arrived three months later, the city had been more or less flattened and its people massacred.

The Russians continued their push towards Germany, which caused panic in the civilian population. The Red Army had a reputation for being brutal—especially in the light of how the German armies had previously treated Russian civilians.

In the North African desert 1942 was also to be the year of reckoning for the Germans. They would push the British back towards Egypt but at El Alamein in October they would be beaten decisively. Here British infantry trains for the battle.

North Africa

When Germany started its offensive in Europe, Mussolini wanted to make some territorial gains too, so he sent his armies into North Africa. They invaded Libya and parts of Ethiopia, but were quickly repulsed by Allied troops. Most of the Italian forces were simple peasant conscripts who just wanted to go home to their farms, so they had little interest in fighting. Hitler had his eyes on the oilfields of the Middle East, and so he sent troops under General Erwin Rommel to back the Italians up. This signalled the start of a bitter war that waged back and forth along the coastline of Egypt and Libya. The Germans lost a major battle at El Alamein in October 1942, from which they never fully recovered. A year later American troops arrived, and together the Allies swept the German armies out of North Africa.

The Allies then built up enough supplies to invade mainland Europe. After deceiving the Germans with fake invasion attempts, the Allies landed in Sicily on July 10, 1944, and within two months proceeded to the southern parts of the Italian peninsula. This caused panic amongst Italy's leaders, and Mussolini was voted out by the Fascist Grand Council, who re-instituted a constitutional monarchy. The King then had Mussolini arrested and imprisoned, and installed Marshal Pietro Badoglio as head of government. The Italian government signed an armistice with the Allies five days after Allied forces had landed on mainland Italy. Hitler was furious, and sent massive German forces to take over defence of the country. A furious series of battles followed which saw the Allies work their way up the Italian peninsula, in the meantime the Allies decided to open up a second front elsewhere..

Allied soldiers working in the El Alamein war cemetery in the wake of General Montgomery's decisive defeat of German and Italian troops in Egypt, October 1942.

British troops keep a watchful eye over Axis PoWs as they are taken back from the front.

Two more photographs of German surrenders in North Africa.

After the Operation 'Torch' landings in Tunisia the Axis forces were slowly squeezed into the tip of Tunisia. Some escaped by air to Sicily; a few tried to escape by water; over 150,000 were taken prisoner.

General Bernard Montgomery (c), commander of the British Army in North Africa during the Western Desert campaign, confers with staff officers, including Lt-Gen Herbert Lumsden, X Corps.

Allied air supremacy was a vital ingredient in the destruction of the Axis forces in North Africa. Here, a train of 26 trucks is left shattered and burning after an attack by long range fighters of the RAF south of Sidi Barrani, Egypt.

The 'Desert Fox'—Erwin Rommel fought brilliantly in the desert. Always short of equipment and troops thanks to the British air and sea blockade of the southern Mediterranean, Rommel left the desert to command Army Group B in France and it was there in July 1944 that he was wounded by an Allied air attack. He was implicated in the July Bomb Plot against Hitler and forced to take his own life.

Japan

Hitler's greatest mistake of World War II took place on December 11, 1941, when he declared war on the United States of America. He did so alongside his ally Japan who, three days earlier, had launched a huge air strike on the U.S. fleet in Hawaii. This infamous attack was an attempt to destroy U.S. seapower in the Pacific at a stroke. Since the US Pacific fleet was stationed at Pearl Harbor, this was a natural place to start. Brilliantly planned and executed, at 7:30 am on December 7, 1941, the Japanese attacked with 350 carrier-launched aircraft from a task force commanded by Admiral Isoroku Yamamoto. Over 2,400 people were killed and eight U.S. battleships were sunk or damaged.

The reasons for Japan's attack on the United States were economic and territorial. A series of American trade embargoes had been in place since Japan had invaded China in 1937, including an initial ban on the sale of aviation fuel and scrap metal. When Japanese forces pushed further and took French Indochina (what is now Vietnam), it was too close to the U.S. dependent Philippines for American comfort, and a further embargo was put on oil. The Japanese needed oil to continue their territorial ambitions, and proposed to get it by invading the East Indies, but before they could do this they had to neutralise of the U.S. Navy, major units of which had been sent to Hawaii to deter Japanese aggression.

Yamamoto's plan may have been a tactical success: strategically, it was a massive failure. The Japanese had not destroyed any of the U.S. Navy's carriers, and it was they that would take the fight to the Japanese. The day after Pearl Harbor the United States declared war on Japan. The same day Hitler ordered the German Navy to attack U.S. warships on sight. World War II had suddenly become global.

Above and Above Left: Pearl Harbor: eight U.S. battleships would be sunk or damaged in the unexpected attack. The top photo was taken by a Japanese aircraft during the attack between 07:55 and 08:05am, when the Arizona *exploded. Oil can be seen gushing from two other battleships—*Oklahoma *and* West Virginia*—from previous torpedo hits, while a bomb explods on* Arizona*'s stern. The bottom half of the photo shows 'Battleship Row' three days later.* Maryland *is moored beside the capsized* Oklahoma. West Virginia *is on the bottom pinning* Tennessee *to the quay and* Arizona *is totally destroyed. Note oil seeping from* Arizona*: it still bleeds oil to this day.*

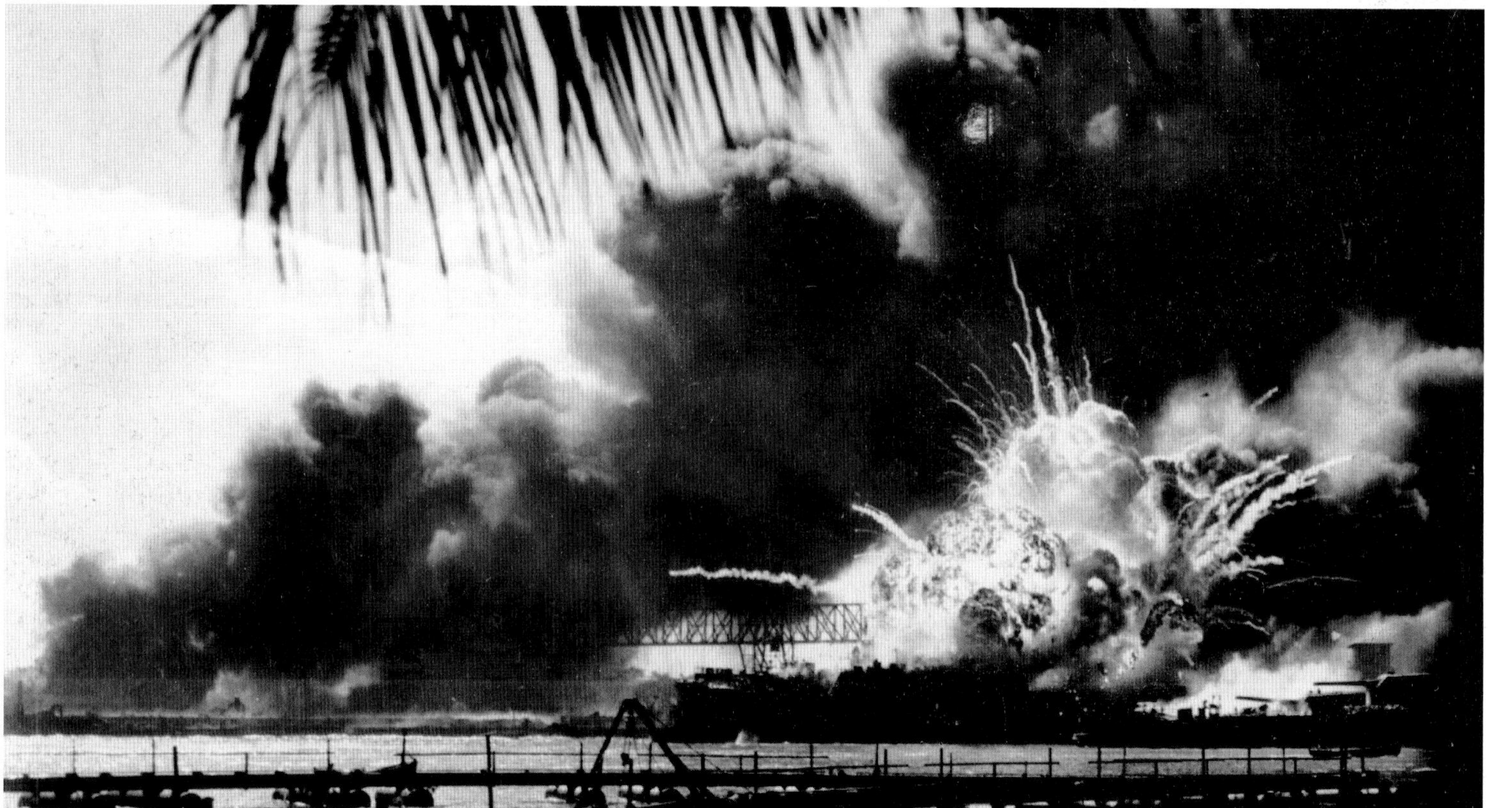

Graphic views of Pearl Harbor. Top, Arizona *burns out of control at right.* West Virginia *(at left), decks awash, sunk at her berth, burns fiercely; in the middle, trapped between the two,* Tennessee. *The lower photograph shows the moment when the destroyer USS* Shaw *exploded.*

Japanese carrier-born aircraft did not just attack American targets in December 1941. On December 9, battleship HMS Prince of Wales *and battlecruiser HMS* Repulse *were both sunk by air attack. Here, Japanese crew watch the take-off of aircraft attacking the British ships.*

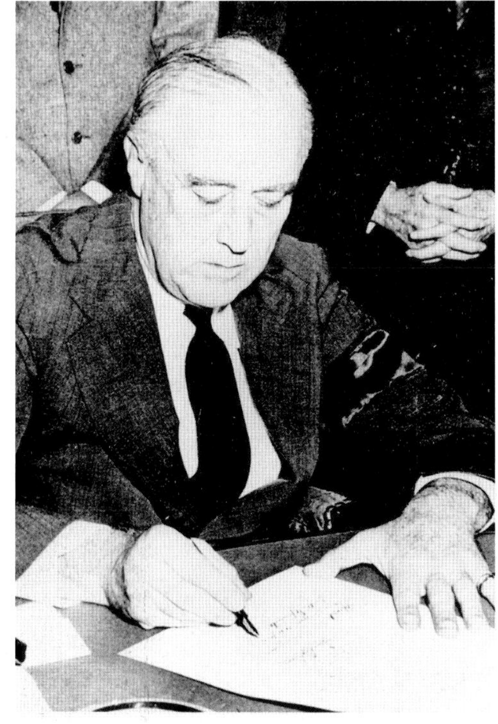

December 8, 1941—Franklin D. Roosevelt signs the declaration of war against Japan.

On April 18, 1942, 16 B-25s led by Lt-Gen Jimmy Doolittle bombed targets in Japan. The military impact was minimal: however the effect of such an operation on Allied morale was incalculable.

Dieppe was an attempt in 1942 to take an enemy-held port to see if this was a suitable way to open up a Western Front. It wasn't. Over two thirds of the force—many of them Canadian—were killed or captured. Instead, the Allies attacked from the south, landing first in Sicily (in July 1943) and then in Italy (in September 1943).

British troops in Italy in late 1943.

The Italian winters can be wet, and mud was a continuous problem in 1943–44.

British Bren gunner in action in Italy.

Italy was supposed to be the 'soft underbelly' of the Axis—it was anything but. Stiff German resistance would ensure that fighting continued until May 1945.

One of the major battles of the Italian campaign took place on the German's defensive Gustav Line in the first half of 1944: Monte Cassino was finally taken in May after massive bombardments had reduced the monastery at the top to rubble.

Heavy snow in Italy in early 1944.

Polish troops spearheaded attacks on Cassino. Here a Polish soldier armed with a Thompson submachine gun cautiously examines a flag of surrender.

Rome was taken in July 1944 after the fall of the Gustav Line.

British antitank gunner in Italy.

U.S. Fifth Army under General Mark Clark was the major American component of the Allied forces in Italy.

British paras before their drop into Normandy on June 5.

D-Day: Operation 'Overlord'

By 1944, the Americans had shipped enough men and equipment across the Atlantic that a fresh Allied offensive aimed directly at Germany was possible. In order to confuse the German High Command as to where the invasion would land, a huge campaign of disinformation was mounted—in this it was particularly successful. An enormous force was assembled under Supreme Allied Commander, Dwight D. Eisenhower, and on June 6, they landed on the Normandy coast. The invasion was codenamed Operation 'Overlord', and since the Germans were expecting the attack to come at Calais, it was relatively unopposed. Nearly a million men were put ashore in the first ten days - this was helped by the French resistance who cut telephone lines and blew up bridges to slow down the German military response.

From this point onwards, the Allies fought their way through northern France, moving towards Germany's borders. Hitler tried one last massive counter-attack when they struck back in the Ardennes in what became known as the Battle of the Bulge. He used all his reserve troops and what was left of the army's equipment, so when the offensive failed, it was effectively all over for Germany. The only issue in doubt was whether the Russians would get there first.

German troops lay mines on the French beaches.

British paras prepare for take-off on June 5. The airborne component of D-Day—including the U.S. 82nd and 101st Airborne Divisions—was significant and did much to disrupt the German defences.

The U.S. forces that landed on Omaha Beach—as so graphically portrayed in the Spielberg film Saving Private Ryan*—had the hardest time on D-Day: there were 2,500 casualties. This was in part due to the fact that the armour support—Shermans fitted with swimming skirts—was disembarked too far from shore and all sank.*

Once the bridgehead was secure, Allied armour was able to wade ashore and help support the infantry.

Omaha beach after resistance had been broken. Note the barrage balloons: in fact, Allied air superiority over the beaches was absolute.

US troops land on Utah beach.

British troops arrive in Normandy.

Reinforcements arrive on Omaha.

Reinforcements would continue to build up in Normandy—they were needed immediately as the Germans threw everything they had at the beachhead in an attempt to sweep the invaders into the sea.

Royal Marine Commandos move off the beach into the bocage of Normandy.

News of the invasion reaches London.

German prisoners, late July 1944.

An American unit passes a clutch of dead enemy.

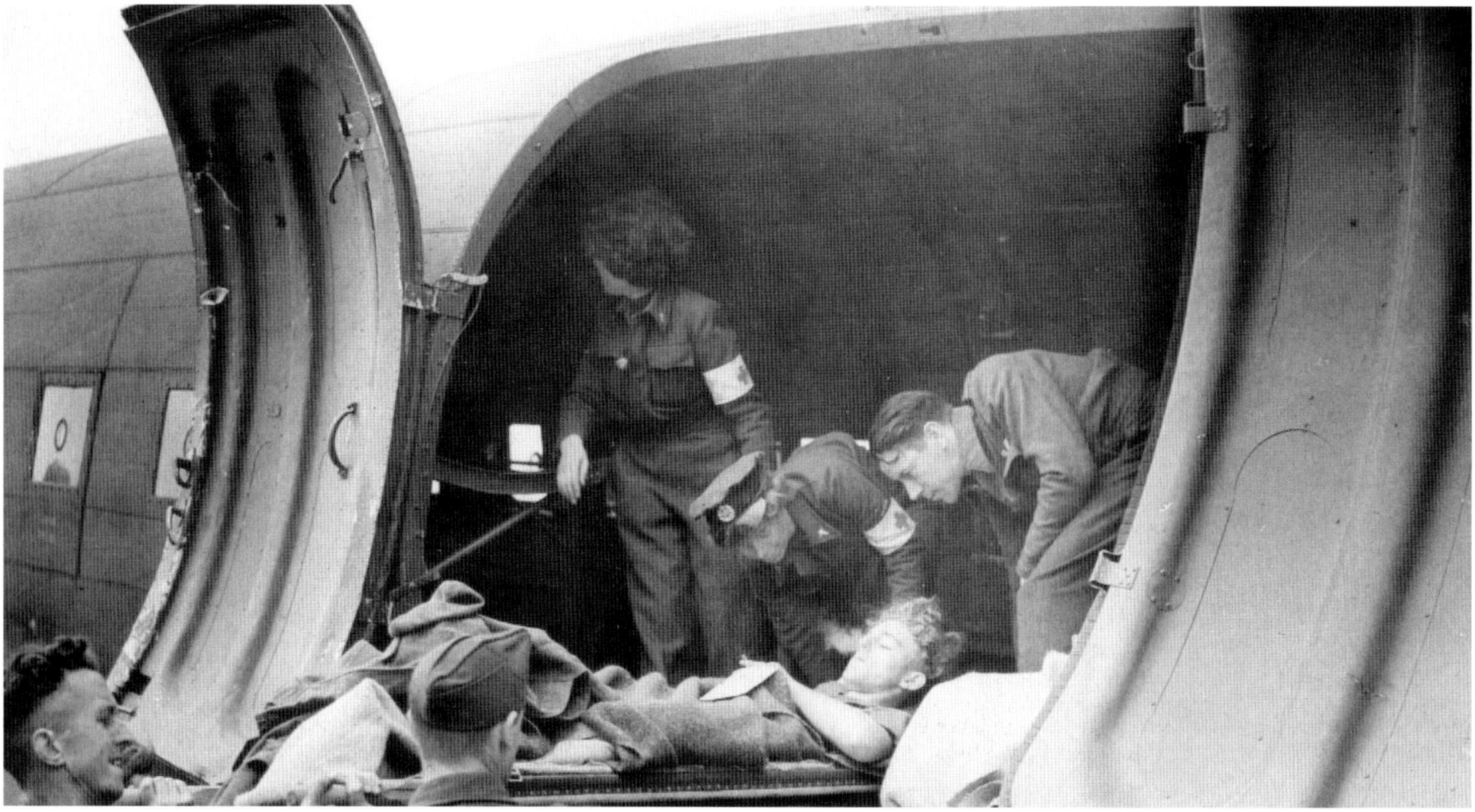

D-Day+7: wounded soldiers are flown back to Britain by Dakota.

Medical provision on the beaches behind the cover of a Churchill AVRE.

June 10, U.S. troops capture a German soldier in Normandy.

Hitler with Keitel and Göring to his right and Bormann to his left after the July 20, 1944, bomb plot. Hitler is holding his right arm, slightly injured in the blast.

U.S. 82nd Airborne Division assault on Nijmegen, September 17, 1944; this is a still from a cinefilm taken of the drop of 1st Battalion 505th Parachute Infantry Regiment. At the centre of the photograph is a supply parapack from a C-47 Skytrain: the colour of the chute would tell whether it contained ammo (red), medical supplies (white), rations (yellow) or equipment (blue).

The End Game

On the morning of July 20, 1944, an attempt to kill Hitler had been mounted by many of his highest-ranking officers. One of them, General Stauffenberg placed a briefcase packed with British made explosives near Hitler during a meeting. The bomb went off, but failed to kill the Führer—with the exception of General Rommel who committed suicide, all the conspirators were executed.

At this stage, Germany was being squeezed from all sides—the Allies had turned their domestic industrial centres into military production systems of awesome capability; Russia had done likewise, and their combined output was staggering. Germany, whose supply chains had been strangled, could not possibly match the hardware that was coming its way; the Third Reich was doomed.

By the end of 1944, the Allies had gained control of France and Belgium, and had entered German soil. Rumania, Bulgaria, and Finland, which had previously been Hitler's allies, all changed sides. The biggest military obstacle for the Allies was the River Rhine—this was easily defended, but after much fighting, American forces got across on March 7th 1945. At the end of April 1945 the Red Army surrounded Hitler's bunker in Berlin, and on April 30, he faced up to reality and shot himself. On May 8, the remaining Nazis surrendered unconditionally.

Photograph taken by a PR Spitfire of British 1st Airborne Division's landing area DZ 'X' outside Arnhem. The airborne landings were part of Operation 'Market Garden'.

The target—the bridge across the Rhine at Arnhem.

One of the problems with the operation was that the German troops on the ground were tougher than expected. These are men of IInd SS Panzer Corps digging in.

These Waffen-SS prisoners are being guarded by glider pilots of No 16 Flight, F Squadron, RAF.

View from the north bank of the Waal River and Nijmegen bridge. US airborne troops completed their part of 'Market Garden' successfully, capturing Eindhoven and Nijmegen bridges.

Above, Below and Above Right: German industry was not put onto a total war footing until 1944, when Allied bombing was growing in intensity. Its armoured vehicle output, therefore, never matched that of the Allies in quantity, although its quality was high. Thus the mass-produced (nearly 50,000) 35-ton Allied M4 Sherman (below, in winter camouflage) was more effective than its bigger and better rivals as exemplified here by the 68-ton King Tiger (above right: less than 500 produced). Also illustrated (above) a 75mm-armed SdKfz 250 armoured car.

The last attempt by Hitler to win the war in the west was the offensive in the Ardennes in December 1944. A costly failure, it used up equipment and troops that could have made the defence of Germany a much harder job, although for a few brief days it shook up the Allies.

Germany in Wartime

At the start of World War II, the standard of living experienced by Germans citizens varied tremendously, depending on race, religion and connections. For those 'fortunate' enough to have close Nazi Party links, life could be very comfortable, but those with 'tainted' blood found themselves in a very different situation. The main tool of public control was terror, and the men of Himmler's SS and Gestapo units were feared through the Reich. People targeted by these units often simply disappeared, never to be seen again. In the early days of Hitler's power they focussed on political activists—mostly Communists and Socialists, but as time went on their place was taken by the Jews and other 'undesirable' groups.

For the average German citizen, however, things were better than they had been for a long time. The Third Reich had provided them with full employment, and there was complete social order. For the first time in years the economy was under control, and there was absolute political stability. Germany had regained her status on the world stage thanks to many things including much improved diplomatic affairs, as well as the well-publicised sporting prowess of her top athletes and motor racing teams.

Goebbels made sure that his propaganda instilled German workers with a sense of pride—they were made out to be heroes in their workplaces, and social projects and leisure programs helped keep morale high. The popular 'Strength through Joy' program gave workers the opportunity to take holidays in Scandinavia, Italy, or Germany.

Incendiaries rain down on Nuremberg, August 28/29, 1942. The bombing campaign would destroy many of Germany's finest cities.

Throughout most of the war the holiday resorts stayed open, and many small hotels were dedicated to a program named KLV, or *Kinderlandverschickung*. This initially provided vacations for children from large industrial towns, but later, as Allied bombing made the cities more dangerous, they were used to evacuate entire schools.

Himmler also made sure that the churches did not overstep the mark—provided that they did not interfere with Nazi matters, they were tolerated. Occasionally, however, the churches did complain, such as when Himmler started to clean up the gene pool by co-ordinating a compulsory euthanasia program for those considered to be mentally deficient. In this instance complaints from the Catholic church were heeded, and the program was halted on August 28th 1941. It should be stated, however, that the Vatican had very little to say about the elimination of the Jews.

The Nazi's purge of dissenting voices had been so successful that the government felt that there was no need to censor the press - non-Nazi newspapers had all but disappeared. In the cinemas Josef Goebbels wanted the German people to see films which continued the party message, and so he maintained a strong influence on their production.

As soon as war broke out in 1939, the government imposed rationing on the people—this was controlled through a ration cards scheme. Every

Into the Reich: in World War I German soil was left untouched, its infrastructure hardly damaged by a few bombs. World War II was different: Hitler proposed a scorched earth policy and vowed to defend the Reich to the last. Here Allied tanks and artillery fire on German troops in Germany itself.

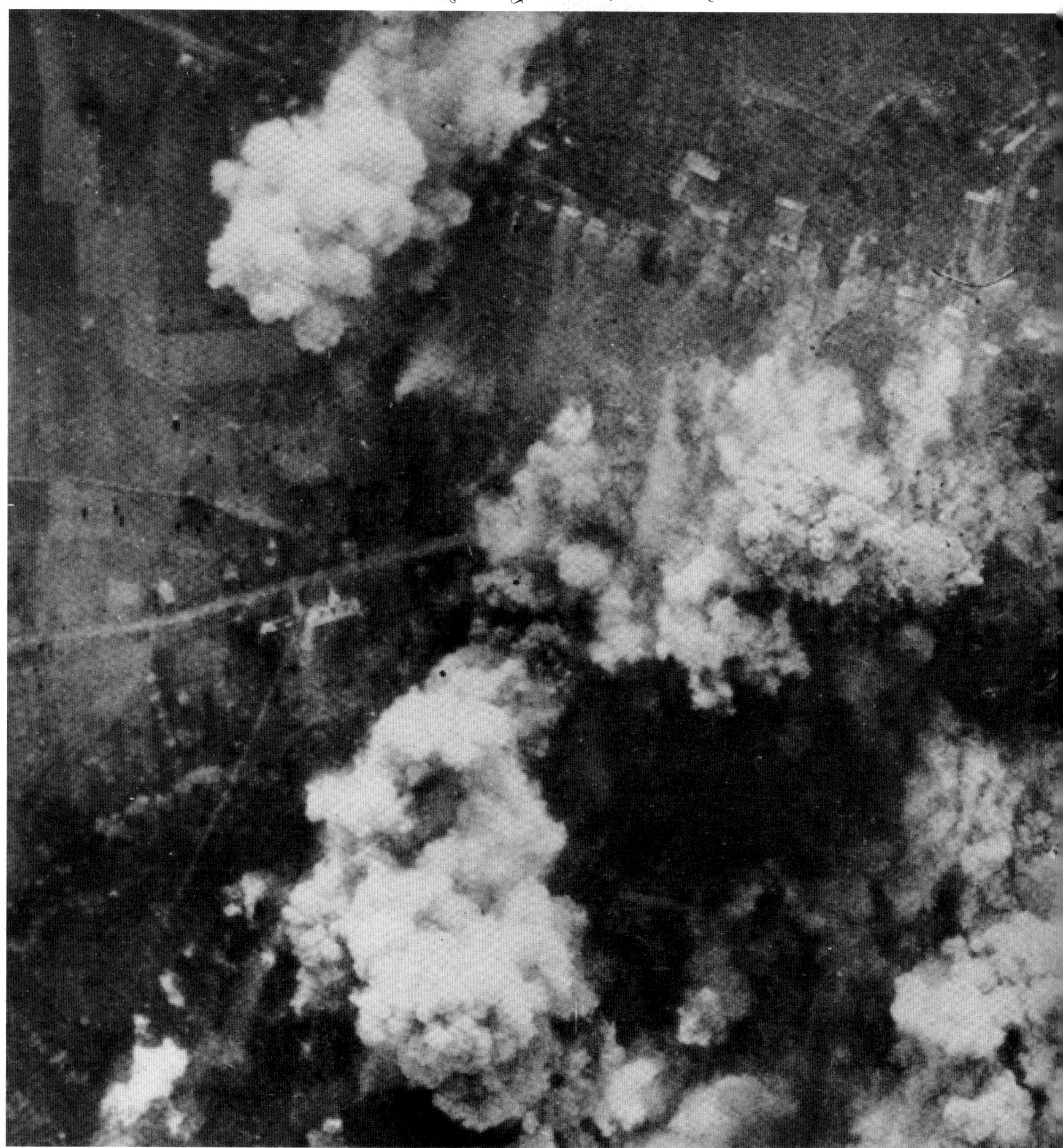

The USAAF by day and RAF by night battered German economy, infrastructure and cities. The strategic bombing campaign caused dreadful damage: Dresden lost some 50,000 civilians in a firestorm created by Allied bombers.

The main RAF bomber of the period was the Avro Lancaster; of the USAAF, the B-17. German fighter and Flak defences ensured that the cost of attrition to aircrew and aircraft was high, but the toll on industry and infrastructure such as railway marshalling yards was higher.

The bombing of the lovely Hanseatic port of Lübeck led to the tit-for-tat 'Baedeker' raids—so called because the targets were chosen for their historical interest: Bath, Canterbury, Exeter, Norwich and York.

The question of the morality of bombing German cities is unlikely to have figured greatly in the minds of the average bomber crew who had lived through the Blitz and the U-boat war. This is the crew of 'G-George' a Lancaster that took part in the raid on Duisberg.

'Germany Forwards!' The Nazi propaganda of the 1930s created a militaristic society that wanted to see Germany rise again following her humiliation at the end of World War I.

person was issued with a paper card which was made up of tokens for specific amounts of the most popular foods as well as for tobacco. While the ration for clothes and shoes was on an individual basis, solid fuels such as coal were distributed by the household. All ration tokens were collected by the merchants or store owners and passed on to the authorities.

On top of rationing, there was recycling—the German government had been encouraging its people to recycle their domestic waste for some years before the war began. This was done to help the German economy, since reusing materials meant that imports could be kept to a minimum. This not only helped financially, but also helped reduce the country's reliance on shipping raw materials through enemy waters. To this end, scrap metals were the most sought after materials, but other items were also collected, including old clothes and bones left over from cooking.

Although the ration limits were adequate to live on, luxuries such as chocolates were unknown for many years. Meat was in short supply, and so was eaten less regularly by most people. Those who performed strenuous physical work did, however, have a larger allowance, whereas children got less. Some foodstuffs such as coffee were not rationed, but were simply unobtainable—this included all the exotic fruits, such as bananas, oranges and lemons. Those items which were locally grown were not limited, so things like apples and potatoes were generally available, depending on the season and the area. Although the black market was widespread in Britain, in Germany it was almost non-existent, since the penalties if caught were severe.

As soon as the war was underway, domestic transport was severely restricted by fuel shortages. All vehicles had to display permits, which were normally only available for industrial or commercial use. Doctors were exceptions to the rule, however, the authorities confiscated many of the better quality cars in private ownership for use by high-ranking military officers. Public rail transport remained unrestricted for most of the war.

In the summer of 1941, Hitler began the Holocaust—his *Einsatzgruppen* death squads ranged through captured territories, identifying and murdering 'undesirables'. These included Jews, political leaders, gypsies and many others—in all, many tens of thousands were killed. The German public remained blissfully unaware of the horrors of the holocaust, however. This was because Josef Goebbels kept up an unceasing propaganda campaign to keep them this way. They were shown bogus films, such as those that portrayed Jews who had been shipped to concentration camps in the east seemingly living happily on farms in good health and spirits. While some Germans guessed the truth, most chose not to think the unthinkable.

Hitler had not planned on a long war—he had told his generals that his armies would be victorious since all would fall before them. Once it became clear that this would not be the case, Germany had to change its industrial priorities and reorganise for full-scale military production. On February 8, 1942, Albert Speer was made Reich Minister of Armaments, and put in charge of the German war production. The output of armaments in particular were massively increased, in spite of the intense Allied bombing raids. Most of the extra labour came from slave workers—some seven million of them, forced out from their homes and into factories which were often thousands of miles away. Vast numbers of these workers died of mistreatment, malnutrition and sickness.

Life was not easy for German civilians who lived in or near any of the towns and cities, especially those which had any kind of industrial capacity. More than 1000 cities and villages were bombed by the Allies, during which nearly a million tons of explosives were dropped. Most of the victims were women, children and the elderly, since those capable of fighting were away at a battle front somewhere. Although it was the Germans who pioneered the use of incendiary bombs, the Allies used them to create fire storms which destroyed the cities of Hamburg, Dresden, Cologne, Essen, Freiburg, and Dortmund. These attacks also left large parts of Berlin and Munich in ruins, and killed 80,000 children among the civilians who perished. They also destroyed some 3.5 million homes and left 7.5 million Germans homeless.

The death toll in Dresden was particularly bad since it was temporarily housing a massive number of refugees who were fleeing from the advancing Red Army. Although it has been claimed that the destruction of Dresden was unnecessary, it was a major communications and transportation centre, and so was of great strategic significance. Churchill also wanted to show the Russians just what the Allies were capable of doing to a city. It is possible that if Dresden had not been so convincingly destroyed, Stalin may not

Much of Germany's armed forces were used as an army of occupation—from Scandinavia to Poland. This German guard is at the entrance to the Storting, the Norwegian parliament.

American nurses at the junction of the Unter Den Linden and Wilhelm Strasse during a tour of the ruined German capital. The massive damage is self-evident.

Around Europe VE (Victory in Europe)-Day, May 8, 1945, men, women and children celebrated the end of the war and the downfall of Nazi Germany.

have stopped at Berlin, and the war may have escalated into a far worse conflict.

As the war progressed, the authorities became ever more oppressive in their attempts to maintain control over the German population. Anyone who questioned the 'final victory' of their country, or was caught listening to foreign news on the radio was executed.

In the closing stages of the war, when Hitler realised that defeat was certain, he decided that all Germany should be destroyed in the classical 'scorched earth' manner as a last act of defiance. He felt that it was what the German people deserved for allowing themselves to be beaten. His words on the matter were:

'We'll not capitulate. Never. We can go down. But we'll take a world with us.'

In March 1945 he sent the order for the destruction of Germany's stores of food, clothing and military equipment, power stations, electrical distribution systems, and all communications centres and transport facilities. Likewise, every factory was to be razed to the ground to stop them falling into the hands of the Allies. Reich Minister of Armaments, Albert Speer tried to persuade Hitler that this would cause even more suffering for the German civilian population, but he was beyond reason, believing they should be punished, saying:

'If the war is lost, the nation will also perish. This fate is inevitable. There is no necessity to take into consideration the basis which the people will need to continue a most primitive existence. On the contrary, it will be better to destroy these things ourselves because this nation will have proved to be the weaker one and the future will belong solely to the stronger eastern nation.'

In April 1945 soldiers from the US 69th Infantry division met up with troops from the Russian 58th Guards division—this effectively cut northern Germany from the south. On April 30, Adolf Hitler knew that the end had come, and committed suicide. An announcement was made to the German people, stating that:

'Our Führer, Adolf Hitler, fighting to the last breath against Bolshevism, fell for Germany this afternoon in his operational headquarters in the Reich Chancellery. On April 30th, the Fuehrer appointed Grand Admiral Doenitz his successor.'

Three days later, on May 2, 1945, the 'Thousand Year' Reich came to an end as the remnants of the German government surrendered. The last days of fighting in Berlin had been some of the most intense of the entire war. On May 4 the German High Command surrendered all their forces in north-west Germany, Holland, and Denmark to Field Marshal Montgomery. Three days later, at General Eisenhower's headquarters in Reihms, Admiral Friedburg and General Jodl officially signed Germany's unconditional surrender to the Allies. Fighting stopped at 12:00 am on the morning of May 9, and across Europe the guns were silenced.

The concentration camps disclosed their dreadful secrets as they were liberated by the Allies, and local Germans were often forced to help with the clearing-up operations by disbelieving troops.

As well as concentration camps there were many slave labour camps throughout Hitler's empire—locations where the enslaved populations of mainly eastern Europe were forced to work until they died.

Ragamuffin children being fed by Allied troops.

THE COST

The actual cost of World War II is incalculable, either in human or financial terms. Estimates indicate that about 55 million people died in Europe during World War II, of these, about 8 million were German.

Death was not just for soldiers—civilians died in their millions too, and came from many different directions through these cruel years. In the opening stages of the war, as the German armies invaded Poland, Hitler wasted little time in organising the killing of large numbers of non-combatants. He wanted to minimise the potential for trouble making amongst the Polish people, and so he tasked Himmler with eliminating the political and cultural elite. Since the job was effectively wholesale murder, it was given to the SS rather than the regular army. Several units of 400 to 600 men were assembled—these were not fighting forces, but death squads. Called *Einsatzgruppen*, their role was to go in after the invading armies had passed and arrest and murder certain categories of civilians. These included government officials, aristocrats, priests, and business people. The squads also sought out Jews and forced them into overcrowded ghettos. The final death toll of Polish Jews was over three million, but another three million or more non-Jewish Polish civilians also died in the war. This amounted to losing around 18% of its pre-war population—this was a greater toll than for any other country in the world.

Over 55 million people died during World War II.

Originally there were plans to ship the German Jews to Madagascar where they would be corralled in special colonies. This became impracticable once war had started, especially when millions more Jews were captured in the occupied countries of the east. Instead, Hitler and Himmler decided that mass extermination was the answer, and so the Holocaust began. The Nazi's 'Final Solution' killed in the order of six million Jews, as well as countless homosexuals, the mentally ill, German political prisoners and Bolsheviks. On top of this, a million Serbs were executed and around 1.5 million Romanies died during the period 1933–1945. It is estimated that the Nazis executed about 12 million civilians in all.

There were death camps at Auschwitz-Birkenau, Belsen, Treblinka, Sobibor, Majdanek, Dachau, Chelmno and many others elsewhere in Germany and Poland. These camps were run by Himmler's Special Duty Section (*Sonderdienst* or SD) who supervised mass exterminations in the killing chambers which they disguised as showers. These had been specially developed to kill large numbers of civilians with a gas called Zyklon-B, a form of cyanide. The dead were then searched for gold teeth; their bodies were often also boiled up to extract fat, which was used to make soap or candles.

At the end of the war these camps were so filled with the dead and the dying that they were serious health hazards to the local population, even after the survivors had been rescued. Belsen, for instance, had to be burned to the ground by British forces with Crocodile flame-throwing tanks to prevent the spread of diseases such as typhus.

As the war progressed, the need for slave labour meant that many of those

Untold millions were damaged by the war—from wounded soldiers to raped civilians.

who were sent to the concentration camps were forced to work in terrible conditions in German armaments factories. Vast numbers died as the result of starvation, disease and maltreatment. As the war drew to a close, the Nazi hierarchy tried to hide evidence of the concentration camps and slave labour units from the advancing Allied armies.

Even as the Red Army reached Berlin, the death toll of non-combatants continued. Not only did the Russians treat the German civilians they encountered with extreme brutality, but the millions of artillery shells that they fired into the city killed nearly a quarter of a million people during the last three weeks of the war. The atrocities the Russians committed on German civilians can be partly explained as revenge for the treatment that Germany troops had exacted on the peasant population of the Soviet Union. The Russians had cause to be bitter for many other reason too, however. In all, about 5 million Russian soldiers were captured by the Germans, but the brutality they experienced at the hands of their captors killed around 3 million of them. The death toll also continued after the war was over—Stalin sent many of them to labour camps for the crime of being captured, where another million of them died. It is thought that the Soviets lost about 13 million soldiers and eight million civilians in all.

All the other countries that were

Wartime economies were wrecked by the war; rationing and shortages continued on into the 1950s. Indeed, it was only the benevolence of the United States' Marshall Plan that enabled the Old World to recover.

So many European economies had been turned over to munitions' manufacture that there would be shortages of many household goods for years to come.

This friendly meeting between East and West near Torgau, Germany, was not continued by the governments of the United States and the Soviet Union postwar: the world polarised down ideological lines.

Massive amounts of money, art treasures and other valuables were looted by the Nazis. The 90th Division discovered this lot in a salt mine in Merkers, Germany.

General Dwight D. Eisenhower, Supreme Allied Commander, accompanied by Gen Omar N. Bradley, and Lt-Gen George S. Patton, Jr, inspects art treasures stolen by Germans and hidden in a salt mine in Germany, April 12, 1945.

Evacuated children enjoy a New Year party in Windsor Castle, 1946.

involved in the conflict lost large numbers of people. Some, like the British also had troops from the Empire and Commonwealth where there was not much fighting on home soil, and so for these countries the civilian toll at 60,000 was low in relation to the 452,000 soldiers killed. Other countries like Czechoslovakia, however, did relatively little fighting, losing 'only' 10,000 soldiers, but they lost an incredible 330,000 civilians. Yugoslavia lost 300,000 fighting men, which was bad enough, but its civilian population experienced a terrible 1,300,000 losses. Many of these occurred when Hitler ordered the destruction of Belgrade in revenge for their brief uprising.

The toll continues—even small countries like Romania lost 200,000 soldiers and 465,000 civilians. British civilian losses at 60,000 were almost entirely due to bombing and rocket attacks, but nearly half a million military men died. Mussolini's eagerness to get involved in the war cost Italy 330,000 soldiers and 80,000 civilians. Hungary for her part lost 120,000 soldiers and 280,000 civilians. France, whose population had been severely depleted in World War I lost a further 250,000 soldiers and 360,000 civilians. Officially the French government also executed 4,500 collaborators, however, an estimated 50,000 more were executed by the French Resistance.

The numbers are so large that they risk becoming meaningless—it is estimated that approximately 25 million soldiers died during the years 1939–45. Of these, some 19 million were killed in Europe, and around 6 million in the war against Japan. The Allied military and civilian losses were in the order of 44 million, and the Axis lost about 11 million. The numbers got much worse in the Far East—the Chinese lost over 11 million to fighting, with up to another 20 million killed by Japanese. The Americans got off relatively lightly—since they experienced no domestic fighting, their civilian losses were insignificant, although they did lose over 400,000 soldiers.

World War II was truly global—in all, 61 countries with 1.7 billion people took part; this amounts to three-quarters of the world's population. 110 million people did military service, with the major participants being the USSR at 22–30 million, Germany at 17 million, the United States at 16 million, the British Empire and Commonwealth at 9 million, Japan at 7 million and China at 5 million.

The financial cost of World War II can only be estimated. It is possible to calculate how much money was spent by the various governments who took part during and after the conflict—some assessments make this figure more than a trillion dollars. This does not, however, take into account the enormous amount of damage done to privately owned property.

The U.S. spent more than any other country, at an estimated $341 billion. This figure includes $50 billion for lend-lease supplies, which is made up of $31 billion to Britain, $11 billion to the Soviet Union, $5 billion to China, and a further $3 billion to 35 other countries. Germany spent $272 billion, the Soviet Union $192 billion, Britain $120 billion; Italy $94 billion and Japan $56 billion. Official Soviet figures show that the USSR lost 30 percent of its national wealth. In total, the war cost Japan an estimated $562 billion.

Headlines from a week's newspapers, April 29–May 5, 1945.

What cannot have a financial value placed on it, however, is the change in the balance of world power. Before the war, there were four great military nations—these were Britain, France, Germany, and Japan.

Although America and the Soviet Union were massive countries, they had small armies. Both had experienced terrible poverty and domestic social problems in the run up to the war as a result of major economic troubles. During the war, however, they built up their military machines to such an extent that when the conflict ceased they stood head and shoulders above everyone else, and the term 'superpower' was coined.

During the war America and the Soviet Union had a common enemy in the Nazis, and they fought together to entirely eliminate the Third Reich. However, this mutual understanding soon evaporated in the post-war era, and matters went downhill rapidly. This resulted in what became known as the 'Cold War', which had a major influence on world politics for several decades thereafter.

In order to punish those responsible for the behaviour of the Third Reich during World War II, a war crimes tribunal was held at Nuremberg between November 1945 and August 1946. Although many senior Nazis had escaped 21 did not, and they appeared before Allied judges to answer charges made to them. Only 3 were acquitted, the other 19 being found guilty. Of these 12 were executed, and 7 were imprisoned .

U.S. Undersecretary of War Robert Patterson visits U.S. 3rd Division at Hitler's guesthouse, Schloss Klessheim, in July 1945. The car is Hitler's 16-cylinder Mercedes tourer seen in earlier chapters.

The documents for the Germans' unconditional surrender have been signed by Alfred Jodl: Eisenhower and other Allied military leaders enjoy the moment at Rheims, France on May 7, 1945.

To a society that was instilled with Nazism, the fall of the Third Reich had a devastating effect—particularly the youngest soldiers such as these Hitlerjugend, here seen being decorated by Hitler on one of his last public engagements.

The Nuremberg War Crimes Trials sat from November 1945 to September 1946 trying 21 senior Nazis for war crimes. This photograph shows the dock—note Göring and Hess at lower left. The verdicts were: death for Göring, Frank, Frick, Jodl, Kaltenbrunner, Keitel, Ribbentrop,

Rosenberg, Sauckel, Seyss-Inquart and Streicher; life imprisonment for Funk, Hess and Raeder; imprisonment for von Schirach (20 years), Speer (20), von Neurath (15), Dönitz (10). Fritsch, von Papen and Schacht were found not guilty.

Deutschland Erwache—Germany Awake.

Hitler
HLAND
CHE

Index